25th September 2014

CW00411559

Steve

FROM THE HEART

STEVE MOREY

For my darling Liz and in memory of
Pops Jenkins, without whom this would
not have been possible.

First published in Great Britain in 2014 by
www.awaywithmedia.com Shrewsbury SY3 7LN

ISBN: 978-0-9576292-7-1

Edited, photographed and published by
Andrew Richardson

Editorial production
Adam Haynes

Preface

We have our customers to thank for *From The Heart*.

For years, our regulars have been asking us to write a book. So, finally, we have.

Our clients wanted to us to explain how they could recreate some of the dishes that they know and love. They wanted to understand more about our food philosophy. And they wanted the secrets of how we take ingredients from nature's larder and turn them into dishes that live long in the memory.

Liz and I live in the undulating Devonshire hills and are inspired each day by our surroundings. We work locally with others who lead similar lives: the farmers and producers who bring thrilling ingredients to our doors.

Liz tells me I have an impressive pedigree – though I leave it for others to make that judgement. Over the years I have been privileged to work for and with some amazing owners, chefs and staff. Even some of the pot-washers would get a well earned place in my dream team. So many have left their mark implanted in my memory. There are so many to thank for this incredible journey I have been on. But I do feel that if I list them all, the recipes and pictures would have to have a book of their own!

My philosophy on food is simple. I am grounded in the classics and I cook with the seasons. Hearty, flavoursome dishes are served with elegance and finesse.

Our book is called *From The Heart* because that is what it is. And it is the way we live our lives. We are proud of every plate that leaves the kitchen and we work tirelessly to create an environment in which our guests can switch off and relax.

There's no artifice and no pretence about what we do. We believe in delivering the highest standards and we are passionate about our work.

In *From The Heart*, we have attempted to capture the essence of our work and provide you with easy-to-follow, user-friendly recipes. We don't believe in making things complicated, or blinding people with science. We've set out recipes that you'll be able to replicate at home.

You don't have to follow everything to the letter. Our intention has been to explain techniques and processes in simple fashion, so that you can adapt our recipes to suit your personal tastes.

Creating our first book was a remarkable and cathartic process. We hope that you enjoy reading it as much as Liz and I enjoyed making it.

STEVE MOREY
April 2014

Contents

Introduction

When people ask me what type of food I cook, I find it difficult to answer. You see, I cook from the heart. I use ingredients that excite me. I create dishes that make people happy.

I'm passionate about local, independent produce. I tend to favour small producers who put love and devotion into their ingredients. My passions aren't a fad or some sort of fashion statement. It amazes me when people jump aboard the 'Buy Local' bandwagon, as though they're leading a revolution. I've always bought local. I've always followed the seasons.

You can go into Escoffier's book and look at the classics and then look at food that people eat in today's restaurants. You'll find very little has changed. I give dishes my own twist, of course, just as all chefs do. But I am an understated chef. I believe in good, honest flavours and classic combinations. I'm an instinctive cook.

I've been asked countless times to create a book. If I had a pound for every time I've been asked to write one . . . as they say. I hope those who have encouraged me will enjoy *From The Heart* – for that is precisely what it is. This is the food that I believe in. These are the dishes that I am passionate about.

Creating my first book was a challenge – not least because I don't use recipes. I must have cooked a million bowls of soup, but I've never once used a recipe. Instead, I use my senses of smell, taste and touch; they tell me when something is right. Trust your own senses when you cook, they won't let you down.

Steve, left, with brothers Andrew and Duncan.

I was born and raised in Paignton, and my wife Liz grew up on a farm just outside Plymouth. Liz attended Plymouth Catering College and I went to South Devon Technical College, which was then based in Torquay.

I'm a townie. My father Reg was in the hospitality industry, as was my mother Jean. Dad was a wine waiter and deputy hotel manager in a three-star seafront hotel in Paignton.

My father tried to steer us away from catering. I guess he didn't want us to suffer from low pay and long, unsociable hours. But it felt entirely natural for me to follow him into the trade.

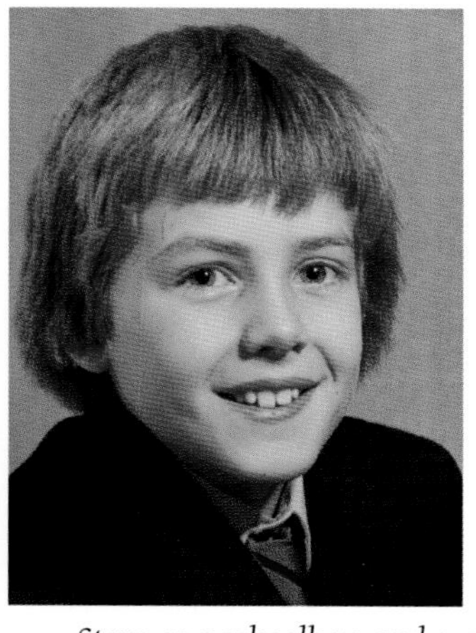

Steve as a schoolboy, and a young Liz helping to bring the cows home . . .

I always enjoyed cooking as a kid. My mother wasn't a great cook, so I used to help out a lot. Mum would leave the sausages on the stove, so they were burned on one side and uncooked on the other. So I'd step up and move them around the pan, so that they were cooked evenly. That's how it all began. Mum and Dad had three boys and I was the middle one. My eldest brother, Andrew, and youngest brother, Duncan, both spent time in hospitality, too.

I cooked when I was still at primary school, making a few biscuits, then in secondary school I loved home economics. I also loved art. I enjoyed drawing and painting. That creative streak serves me well when I present food in my restaurant.

As a kid, there was always food on the table. We were brought up on dishes that were cheap. Dad used to grow a lot of vegetables and also fish regularly. We'd go with him to Paignton, Torquay, Brixham, anywhere on the south coast. We'd catch mackerel during the summer or pollock during winter. I remember Dad filleting a mackerel and cooking it in a pan, then putting a bit of vinegar on it. It was fresh from the sea. The taste was phenomenal.

Dad used to make his own fishing floats and fishing weights. Him and Mum were always doing what they could to make ends meet and take care of their family.

Liz was an only child and used to spend a lot of time out in the fields with her Dad. There was a hotel just up the road from where she lived and she got her first job there. I'm not sure that her Mum and Dad wanted her to work there because they know how unsociable farming was and that the hospitality industry could be even more difficult. But she wasn't put off.

Liz and her Dad on holiday, with Highland cattle.

Liz's parents, Edward and Margaret, enjoyed good food. Margaret was a particularly good cook and Liz enjoyed baking with her. But Liz learned at college that she didn't enjoy the commercial kitchen environment and she decided to make a career in the front of house.

Liz and I met in 1986, in Ascot, at the Royal Berkshire Hotel. It was Ladbroke's flagship hotel, a beautiful Queen Ann mansion. I was on my second job. I'd started out at the Lygon Arms, in Broadway, near Worcester. I spent three-and-a-half years there and was convinced we were cooking the best food in the world. My eyes were opened when I arrived at the Royal Berkshire Hotel. I realised how much I had to learn. My head chef was a phenomenal cook – though his management skills left a lot to be desired. The most important lesson I learned from him had nothing to do with food. He taught me that being aggressive with staff gets you nowhere – and I've always strived to be a decent man in the hothouse of the kitchen.

Liz and I spent a year-and-a-half at the Royal Berkshire. I left in November 1987 along with the sous chef, Richard. We both went to the Lords of the Manor Hotel, at Upper Slaughter, and Liz followed. She knew the manager at the hotel and he was keen to hire her.

The Royal Berkshire Hotel, Ascot.

The three of us were supposed to start work on the same day, but things didn't pan out. The night before we were due to start, Liz, Richard and I attended a party because we'd won an RAC Blue Ribbon Award. There was a staff party at a hotel in Windsor and the chef, Jonathan, sat me next to an open fire and plied me with brandy and champagne. I thought I was fine until I went outside to get a little fresh air: then – *bam*! – it hit me. I was very ill. I was almost arrested and thrown in jail, but a very good friend took me away and made sure I was okay. When I woke up the following morning, I felt felt as bright as a button. But then I tried to move my arms and legs – they were stuck. I was wide-eyed and legless and I couldn't make it into work.

I made it in the following day and Liz and I stayed

Liz and friends at Gravetye Manor.
Bottom: Steve, brother Duncan and chef friends at Gravetye Manor.

for a year. I was offered a return to the Royal Berkshire and asked to start a month before Christmas. On my first day, I worked in the kitchen and Norman, the head chef, welcomed me into the kitchen before disappearing to a management meeting. He told me he'd be gone an hour – but that was the last I ever saw of him. He was sacked on the spot, I've no idea why. That left the sous chef, a guy called Lief, to run the kitchen. Leif was from Denmark and knew nothing about traditional British food. So he was given a month off. That meant I was in charge for the busiest month of the year. I had two choices: sink or swim. It was a big, busy hotel with more than 100 bedrooms and plenty of functions. I spoke to the seven guys in the kitchen and they backed me. So I stayed for a frenetic month before deciding to move on. I've always been a grafter. Hard work is almost a religion. That difficult month taught me that I could cope with adversity. All you have to do is get your head down, do what you can and push on.

The new year brought a new job, this time near East Grinstead at Gravetye Manor. It was the UK's second country house hotel, after Sharrow Bay in the Lake District. I went to Gravetye as the second chef. It was a Relais & Chateaux hotel and the standards were high. Liz was offered a job on reception and stayed for six years.

My head chef was called Mark Raffan. He was a super guy, though there were times when he seemed to spend as much time out of the kitchen as he did in it. I held the fort for a long time and stayed for 18 months. Mark spoke frequently about his plans to move on, but after a while I realised he was in no rush and so I decided to seek new challenges.

I responded to a job advertisement for a chef on a private touring train in Scotland. It was a completely leftfield thing to do but it turned out to be an inspired

"The head chef welcomed me into the kitchen before disappearing to a management meeting. He told me he'd be gone an hour – but that was the last I ever saw of him."

move. The train was a little bit like the Orient Express. It catered for 32 people and had 14 staff. I'd been in hotels for a few years and it was great to do something different. My head chef Graeme and I had similar ethics and it was great fun for a year. At the end of the season, Graeme told me he was leaving. I was interviewed for the top job and given an offer. But then Graeme changed his mind. I hit the road, rather than stay. It had been a great year and I didn't want things to spoil.

I worked at Sud Ouest for a while and then heard a whisper that Mark was leaving Gravetye. I was interviewed for the head chef's job and offered it on the condition that I spend a few months working at Le Gavroche, with the Roux brothers.

Lifetime friends, Dianne and Graham with Liz and Steve, enjoying a day-long picnic.
Left: Steve on The Royal Scotsman.

I signed up for eight months there, working with Michel Roux Jr and Albert Roux. I was 26 at the time and relatively experienced compared with some of the other guys in the kitchen. On my first day, I was working on the chopping block with Michel Roux Jr, who is Albert's son. Albert had strong connections with Gravetye Manor and knew me already. He walked into the kitchen on that first morning and threw his arms around me. "Steve, my boy," he said. "Welcome." All the other chefs looked up and seemed to think: "He's only been here for five minutes, what the hell's going on?" You can imagine how much stick I got for that.

Michel Roux Jr and Mark Prescott were Le Gavroche's head chefs and we were largely left to our own devices. My first section was sauce, where I had to learn from a guy called Max. But after three days Max was called off. "Right Steve, you're on your own, off you go." It was a character-building time.

Eight months later, I started as head chef at Gravetye. There was a lot of responsibility. Liz was still there and I stayed in post for three-and-a-half years. I took the job as far as I could and gave all I had to give. One of the big focuses for the hotel was winning a Michelin star, but I've never been one to go out looking for accolades. If they come along, then great. But creating great flavours has always been more important to me than trying to win awards.

Leading the kitchen in a busy hotel involves spending a lot of time in management meetings and not enough cooking. I loved to cook, but I didn't enjoy the internal politics. Every six weeks, I'd create a new menu for the hotel owner. It would be ticked and crossed like a school report and then I'd have to cook all of the dishes for the hotel managers, who would mark them out of ten. It was like being back in the classroom.

I was nearing 30 and it was time to spread my wings.

After a short spell at Bradford-on-Avon I went to a hotel called Homewood Park Hotel, just outside Bath. Liz and I had married in 1995, at Holbeton, just outside Plymouth, and were on the property ladder. We were happy in our personal lives but Homewood was far from being the job of my dreams.

Liz, Steve and families on their wedding day.

Steve and friends at the New Inn, Coln St Aldwyns.

After a while, I went for lunch with an old friend at the New Inn, at Coln St Aldwyns. It was a quintessential English village, one of the prettiest and most desirable in the UK. The New Inn was clad in ivy and had a special atmosphere. It was looking for a new chef and the owner, Brian Evans, introduced himself. We had a chat and I thought nothing more of it.

But a few hours later, the phone rang. It was Brian. He said: "Was our little chat an interview?" I said: "No." And he said: "Well, how about we do it properly then?" So I went back the following day and he offered me the job.

I really liked the place, there was something about it. I had a great time and the pub became one of the Cotswolds' most popular venues. It had a terrific reputation. I felt really comfortable with the food: it was good and honest and people loved it.

Every chef dreams of owning their own restaurant and after three years at The New Inn, Liz and I started to look for properties. It was time for us to create a restaurant of our own.

It took us three years to find Blagdon Manor. We'd looked at all sorts of properties and endured a torrid time with estate agents. On one occasion they sent us to a restaurant with a giant plastic cactus outside. After a while, we got so fed up that we stopped telling them we wanted a restaurant – every time we did the price seemed to go up.

Liz and I both wanted to come home, to Devon. And then we found Blagdon.

It had been advertised in the *Western Morning News* and was beyond our budget. Liz was keen to view it and after a few days, she won and we came to have a look. The restaurant and hotel had failed. The books were dreadful and the barn, which is now our home, was derelict.

It was advertised as being a house. However, when we arrived to view it there was a sign saying 'hotel'. We couldn't believe it.

Everything seemed to conspire against us. It was the summer of foot-and-mouth disease, so the countryside was in meltdown. And once we'd had an offer accepted, the bank pulled out at the 11th hour, leaving us high and dry.

But we stuck at it and moved in on May 2, 2001. It was the property of our dreams and we worked harder than we've ever worked before to make it a success.

We refurbished the rooms and rebuilt the kitchen, ripping out the old Formica tops and electric oven. Gradually, we turned it around. We removed lath-and-plaster walls, renovated the barn and created an idyllic retreat for our guests.

Today, Blagdon Manor is firmly on the map. We have remarkably loyal guests, who appreciate the relaxed ambience and contemporary cuisine. At Blagdon Manor, we've created a venue that has all of the high standards that you would expect from the best hotels, but without any of the stuffiness or formality.

There's something about the hotel that people love. I remember the first time we walked through the doors, it felt as though a big pair of arms threw themselves around us to offer a big, hearty welcome. Our guests feel the same way. There's just something about the house. It's almost indescribable.

Liz's gran, Pops Jenkins, with Liz's parents at Bibury in the Cotswolds.

Liz and Steve at Blagdon Manor.

As soon as our guests walk in the door, their shoulders drop and they become an inch taller. They seem to let out a great breath as they start to relax.

Some guide books describe my food as being inspired by the French classics; others call it modern British cuisine with a twist. But I think of it as soul food. I cook from the heart. I wear my passions on my sleeve. I love good, honest food. There are remarkable producers in Devon and I am very respectful of their ingredients.

The dishes and techniques that I am sharing with you are intended to bring joy. I hope my philosophies on food – of sourcing the best ingredients and treating them with respect, and of matching complementary flavours and presenting dishes with flair – will resonate with all of you.

From The Heart has been a lifetime in the making. You don't have to follow my recipes to the letter. Use them as a source of inspiration and do as I do: cook from your heart.

SAVOURY

Over many years, I've learned what people like most about canapés: they want them to be playful and they want them to be fun. Our customers expect them to be bursting with flavour and hint at what is to come.

But we've also learned a very important lesson about canapés: less is often more.

People don't want to be full before they've even begun their dinner, and they don't want to be bamboozled with food that is all sizzle and no steak.

So our canapés follow a traditional route. They pack a punch when it comes to flavour, but they are not over the top.

I've put together a series of relatively simple recipes that you'll be able to follow at home. They'll deliver time after time . . . after time.

Sea-salt-and-rosemary nuts

80g whole almonds
80g brazil nuts
1 dsp honey
5g Maldon sea salt
1 dsp sesame oil
2 sprigs rosemary, leaves only, finely chopped

Mix the honey and nuts so that the nuts are evenly coated, and tip into an ovenproof dish. Cook at 180C for five to six minutes or until golden in colour. Remove from the oven and tip into a bowl. Drizzle with sesame oil. When cooled add salt and rosemary and combine evenly. Store in an airtight jar.

Black pudding Scotch eggs

MAKES 6

6 quail's eggs
100g pork sausage meat
50g black pudding, grated
100g seasoned flour
1 egg, beaten
100g white breadcrumbs

Bring a pan of salted water to the boil and cook the eggs for two-and-a-half minutes. Take them straight out of the water and refresh in a bowl of ice-cold water. Once cold, peel the eggs and drain on kitchen paper.

Mix the sausage meat and black pudding together with a little salt and pepper. Divide the mix into six equal portion. Pat each portion out into a flat disc in the palm of your hand and then encase a quail egg, making sure that the egg is completely enclosed. Repeat with all of the eggs. Put in the fridge to set for 10 minutes.

Pass each one through seasoned flour, beaten egg and then breadcrumbs. Deep-fry at 180C for between 90 seconds and two minutes, or until golden.

Drain on kitchen paper, sprinkle with a little salt and serve.

Cheese straws

MAKES APPROXIMATELY 50

100g self-raising flour
75g hard cheese, grated
50g butter
1 egg, beaten
Pinch of salt
Dab of English mustard

Mix the flour, salt and mustard together. Rub in the butter. Add in the cheese and the egg. Mix to a dough.

Roll out thinly and cut into strips of equal length. Place on a greased baking sheet or non-stick mat and cook at 180C for 10 minutes or until golden.

Anchovy sticks

MAKES APPROXIMATELY 30

1 packet pre-rolled puff pastry
12 anchovy fillets
1 egg, beaten

Roll out the pastry to approximately 18cm × 32cm. Cut in half, to give you two pieces measuring 9cm × 32cm.

Brush one sheet with beaten egg and lay 12 anchovy fillets on top, in three rows, leaving space between. Lay the top sheet on top of the bottom. Press down to stick them together but don't squash the anchovies. Cut into thick strips with each strip having three pieces of anchovy in it. Place on a baking sheet and cook at 180C for seven or eight minutes, or until golden.

Serving suggestion. You can use marinated anchovies or, for a stronger taste, salted anchovies.

Tempura of baby corn

MAKES 6

6 baby corn
50g tempura flour
90ml light beer or fizzy water

Bring a pan of salted water to the boil and blanch the corn for a minute. Remove and refresh in ice-cold water. Drain on kitchen paper.

Mix the tempura flour with either beer or water to a smooth batter. Coat the corn in the batter and deep fry at 180C until golden in colour. Drain on kitchen paper and sprinkle with salt. Serve either on their own or with sweet chilli dipping sauce.

Serving suggestion. You can put a little chilli into the batter if you want a spicier twist; you might also use different vegetables such as broccoli, cauliflower or asparagus.

Goujons of sole

MAKES 36

6 fillets lemon sole
100g seasoned flour
1 egg, beaten
100g white breadcrumbs

Cut each lemon sole fillet into six strips. Pass each one through seasoned flour. Pat to remove excess flour.

Pass through beaten egg and then breadcrumbs. Roll the strips on a board with your fingers to make them all even.

Deep fry at 180C until golden and crisp.

Serving suggestion. You can use other fish, though generally softer fish is better. The crunch from the breadcrumbs perfectly compliments the texture of the delicate flesh.

Beetroot relish samosas

MAKES 6

3 sheets of ready-to use-filo pastry
6 tsp beetroot relish (see page 91)
50g melted butter

Lay the first sheet of filo pastry on your work surface and brush with melted butter. Lay the second sheet of filo on top and brush again with butter, before finishing with a third sheet of pastry. Don't butter the top sheet.

Cut the pastry into six equal strips. Put a teaspoonful of relish at the bottom corner of one strip and fold over into a small triangle, leaving the remaining length of the filo intact. Now make further triangular folds up the length of the filo, keeping the triangle shape. Before making the final fold, brush the underside of the pastry with a little butter and then fold and cut away any excess pastry. Repeat for the other samosas.

Place onto a baking tray and cook at 180C for 10–12 minutes or until golden.

Soups are one of the foods I really enjoy making. I think about them all the time, whereas some chefs I have worked with don't put any passion into them. For me it is a completely different story.

I like to extract as much flavour as I can from all the hidden ingredients that support the main act. I also like to cut the ingredients relatively small, so that I can cook the soup quickly. If the dish takes too long to cook, the ingredients can develop a stewed flavour.

A bowl of warming soup, fresh bread and salted butter makes the perfect lunch . . . you don't need anything else.

Before I go any further in this section, I must let you into a secret. Since leaving college, I have never used a recipe for soup. These, therefore, are the first that I have created in my career.

I always cook my soups from the heart and I shall continue to do so, checking the taste every step of the way.

So go on, have a go. Trust yourselves and trust your tastebuds.

Happy Souping!

Roasted squash, Cheddar and rosemary

SERVES 12

1 medium butternut squash, peeled, halved and deseeded
2 tsp honey
1 medium onion, skinned and finely diced
1 carrot
1 sprig of thyme
2 bayleaves
2 rashers of streaky bacon
1 tsp ground cumin
2000ml ham stock or chicken stock
100g Cheddar – just a suggestion: use as much or as little as you like
1 sprig of rosemary – again, you might like more or less
Salt and pepper

With a drizzle of honey, roast the squash in the oven at 170C until slightly golden. Do not burn. Sweat the onion, carrot, thyme, bayleaves and bacon until soft. Add the salt and pepper.

Add the oven-roasted squash, cumin and stock and bring up to the boil. Turn down the heat and simmer until soft. Check the seasoning. Remove the bayleaves and liquidise the soup. Pass through a fine sieve.

Serving suggestion. Serve hot, or refrigerate until you want to use. You can freeze until a later date. When serving, reheat the soup and add grated Cheddar and chopped rosemary.

Asparagus

SERVES 12

200ml olive oil
200g onion
500g fennel
2 bayleaves
2 sprigs of thyme
150g streaky bacon
1 clove garlic
2kg asparagus, peeled and with the tips cut off for later use
500ml white wine
250ml Noilly Prat
3000ml chicken stock
1500ml double cream
Salt and pepper

Sweat the onion, fennel, bayleaf, thyme, bacon, garlic and the bottom stalks of the asparagus with salt and pepper and 200ml of olive oil. To sweat means to cook without colour, on a low heat. Use a lid while cooking: the steam will rise to the underneath of the lid and drops back down, helping the ingredients to cook.

Add the white wine and Noilly Prat and reduce by three quarters. Add the stock and reduce by half. Add the cream and bring to the boil. Reduce and simmer for about two minutes. Put in the raw asparagus tips and cook until tender. Liquidise and pass through a fine sieve. Can be served hot, or in the summer it is nice chilled.

Watercress and potato

SERVES 10

2500ml water
350g potatoes
Salt and pepper
450g watercress
1 tbsp olive oil

Cook the potatoes in water with salt and pepper. Fry the watercress in the olive oil. This is to seal the chlorophyll into the leaves. Add into the water and potatoes. Liquidise and pass through a sieve.

If you want to serve your soup chilled, chill as quickly as possible to keep it green. If you want to serve it hot, either serve straight way or chill and reheat when you are ready.

Serving suggestion. You can serve this soup with crème fraîche and nutmeg croutons. Fry the croutons and toss them in a little ground nutmeg.

Curried parsnip and apple

SERVES 12

1 stick celery, chopped
1 medium-sized onion, finely chopped
500g parsnips, peeled and roughly chopped
1kg Bramley apples, weighed after peeling, cored and diced
60g butter
1 tsp ground curry powder
1 tsp ground cumin powder
60ml cider
1500ml chicken stock
90ml double cream
Salt and ground black pepper

Sweat the celery, onion, parsnips and apple in the butter until soft, with the salt and pepper. Do not colour.

Add the curry powder, cumin powder, cider and chicken stock. Bring to the boil. Turn down the heat and simmer until all the vegetables are soft. Add the double cream and simmer for two or three minutes. Adjust seasoning. Liquidise and pass through a fine sieve. Serve while hot or place in a suitable container refrigerate until required.

Serving suggestion. If you prefer a coarse soup, do not pass it through a sieve.

Lentil

SERVES 12

1 medium-sized onion, finely chopped
2 bayleaves
1 sprig of thyme
1 rasher of smoked bacon, finely chopped
1 garlic clove, finely chopped
1 carrot, peeled and chopped
2000ml ham or chicken stock
½ tsp ground cumin
½ tsp ground coriander
325g lentils – use lentils du Puy, red lentils
200ml olive oil

Sweat the onion, bacon, garlic, carrot, bayleaves and thyme in the olive oil, with salt and pepper. Add the lentils, cumin, coriander and stock. Bring to the boil. Turn down the heat and simmer until the lentils are soft, which should take 35-40 minutes. Adjust the seasoning.

Remove the bayleaves and liquidise the soup. If you like your soup smooth then pass through a sieve; if you prefer a bit of texture, omit this.

Serving suggestion. Serve while hot or chill for later use. Sprinkle with freshly chopped coriander.

Leek and potato

SERVES 6

3 leeks, cut up small – keep the dark green parts for later use
400g potatoes, peeled and cut into small pieces
1 stick celery, cut small
1 medium onion, peeled and cut small
1 garlic clove, peeled and chopped
60g butter
600ml ham or chicken stock
1 bayleaf
1 sprig of thyme
2 rashers of streaky bacon, cut up small
Salt and pepper
200ml double cream

Sweat the whites of the leeks, celery, onion, garlic, bacon, bayleaf and thyme, with salt and pepper, until soft. Add the potatoes and stock and bring to the boil.

Turn down and simmer until the potatoes are cooked. Fry the dark green of the leeks in olive oil to seal in the chlorophyll. Do not brown. Keep the leeks moving all of the time until slightly wilted. Add the potatoes and stock and check the seasoning. Cook until the green leek is soft, but do not cook for too long otherwise it will lose its colour. Liquidise and pass through a fine sieve.

Mushroom

SERVES 8

1 medium onion, chopped
2 leeks, chopped
2 garlic cloves, optional
50g butter
2 tsp olive oil
500g mushrooms – medium-sized flat, peeled and chopped
2–3 sprigs of thyme
1 rasher of bacon, chopped small
600ml ham or chicken stock
400ml double cream

Sweat the onion, leek, garlic, thyme and bacon in the butter and olive oil, with salt and pepper. Add the mushrooms and stock and bring to the boil. Turn down and simmer. Cook until the mushrooms are soft. Add the double cream and bring back to the boil, turn down and simmer for about five minutes. Check seasoning.

Liquidise in a blender and pass through a sieve if you like your soup smooth; if you prefer a coarse texture, omit this.

Serving suggestion. Serve while hot, topped with crème fraîche or yoghurt and chopped chives. A few pieces of scrumpled bacon also works well.

Chilled melon

SERVES 4

2 Charentais or Ogen melons, peeled, deseeded and chopped
100ml sorbet syrup (see page 120)
1 lemon, juice only
¼ water melon, peeled, deseeded and chopped
1 tbsp fresh ginger, peeled, grated and squeezed – juice only
100ml white wine
Handful of fresh strawberries, diced
Small bunch fresh garden mint, finely chopped

Put all the ingredients into a liquidizer and purée until smooth. Pass through a fine sieve. Put into a suitable container and chill until ready for use. When ready to serve, garnish the bowl with diced strawberries tossed in chopped garden mint and then pour over the chilled soup, trying not to disturb the garnish in the bottom.

Serving suggestion. Serve the bowls of soup to your guests and then pour a little Champagne into the bowl. This makes a great talking point and is a lovely way to start a meal. You can also serve in a glass if you prefer.

Basic white bread dough

MAKES 2 LARGE BLOOMERS

680g strong white flour
15g fresh yeast
28g sea salt
28g sugar
150ml rapeseed oil (Cornish for preference)
300ml water

Place the flour into the bowl of your mixer (fitted with a dough-hook attachment) along with the sea salt. In a separate bowl, add yeast and sugar and work to a paste.

Combine the oil and water and warm to 42C. Then add the liquid to the yeast paste and mix; this should now be at 37C, which is the optimal temperature for the yeast to work. (If the temperature is too high it will kill the yeast; if it is too low it takes too long and stunts growth.) To that, stir in four tablespoons of flour and dust the top with a little more. Place somewhere warm for the yeast to start to ferment.

Once it has fermented, or nearly reached the top of the bowl, add the yeast to the flour in your machine bowl. Mix on speed 1 to form a dough. If the mix is a bit dry add water a little at a time; if it is too wet add a little flour.

Once you are happy with the consistency, turn the machine up to speed 2 and mix for five minutes. Empty the mix onto a working surface and divide into two. Roll out into a long oblong, using a rolling pin. Now roll up gently, as though making a sausage shape, pressing down the leading edge, to form two bloomers. Place onto a baking sheet or non-stick mat.

Score the top and cover with a slightly damp tea towel. Leave to double in size. Brush with milk and dust with a little extra flour, then bake at 175C–180C for 25 minutes. Once cooked take off the tray and put onto a wire rack to cool.

All you need now is a big knob of butter. Enjoy!

Note: See the step-by-step guide on page 32.

Basic granary bread dough

MAKES 2 LARGE BLOOMERS

450g strong white flour
450g granary flour
28g sea salt
55g black treacle
150ml rapeseed oil
115g fresh yeast
300ml water

The method is exactly the same as for white bread, but using the black treacle with yeast instead of sugar.

Soda bread

MAKES 2 LOAVES

340g wholemeal flour
340g strong bread flour
40g butter, melted
2 tsp bicarbonate of soda
1 tsp salt
1 tsp cracked black pepper
600ml natural yoghurt

Preheat oven to 180C. Put both flours, butter, bicarbonate of soda, salt and pepper into a large bowl. Stir in the yoghurt and use your hands to mix together until a soft dough forms.

Divide the dough and make into two loaves. Put on to a baking sheet. Cut a deep cross on the top, brush with milk and dust each loaf with flour. Bake for 40-45 minutes until risen and golden brown. Transfer to a wire rack to cool.

Breadmaking: step by step

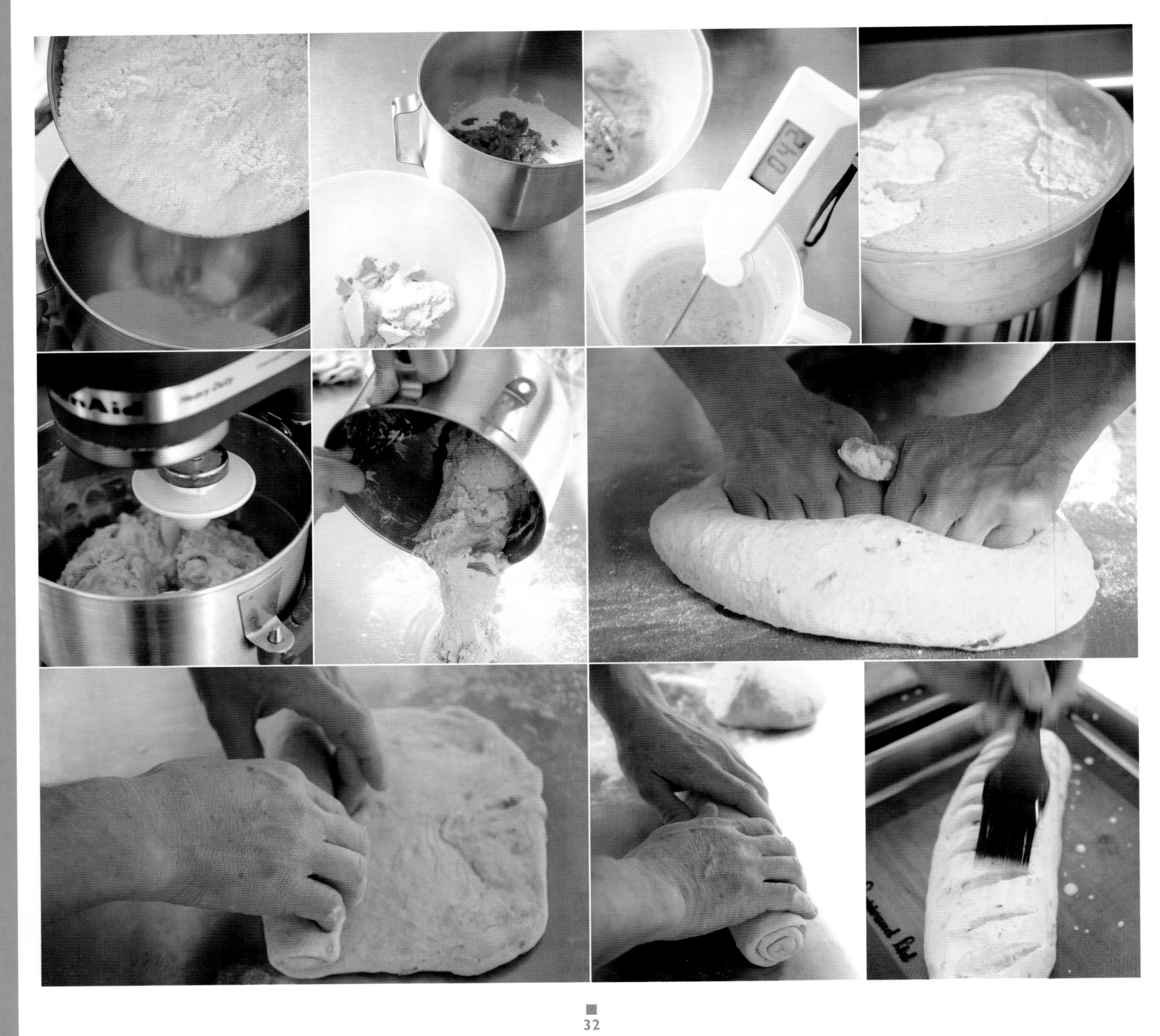

Sun-dried tomato

Add 150g of sun-dried tomatoes in oil, chopped either by hand or in small food processor. Mix into to your flour mix in your machine.

NB: This is the loaf pictured in the step-by-step guide opposite.

Rosemary and sea salt

Use 55g sea salt as opposed to the 28g in the standard recipe.

Add two large sprigs of rosemary, leaves removed and stalks chopped, to the flour at the beginning.

You can add more or less rosemary, if you prefer.

Black pudding

Add 300g black pudding (100g of it grated, the remainder cut into rustic chunks). The grated black pudding is added to your flour mix at the beginning; the chunks go on your rolled-out dough, just before you start to roll into a bloomer.

Mixed seed

Add 25g poppy seeds, 25g sesame seeds and 25g linseed into your flour mix at the beginning.

Mixed olive

Add 150g marinated mixed olives, chopped either by hand or in a small food processor. Add to the flour mix in your machine.

Caramelised onion and goat’s cheese

Heat 50ml of rapeseed oil in a thick-bottomed, non-stick pan and then add one onion, peeled and thinly sliced. Cook on a low heat until soft and translucent. Turn up the heat and carry on cooking until the natural juices begin to caramelise. Take out of the pan and place in a colander to drain. Allow to cool before adding to the flour mix at the beginning.

Add 200g of goat’s cheese (preferably soft and creamy and in rustic chunks) onto the rolled-out dough just prior to rolling into the bloomer shape.

Our great friends Sue and Malcolm are the reason why Devon is such a beautiful and remarkable place. They farm 225 acres, a short distance from Blagdon Manor. They are among the hardest-working, most honest and most genuine people that you could ever hope to meet.

We admire Sue and Malcolm not only because they are among the kindest and best-humoured people we know.

We also admire them because of the work they put into their lives. Farming is a tough occupation and yet they work their socks off to get the best from their land. They keep a small number of pigs as well as lambs and cows.

They frequently work from dawn until dusk, tending the land and making sure their animals lead the best lives possible.

Their food is sensational. Sue and Malcolm grow their own vegetables and formerly ran a small shop, for locals. They also make their own bacon and sausage, as well as curing their own air-dried ham. And they don't mess about with ingredients, either. Their food is good, honest home-cooking that is rustically served and is big on flavour.

During the game season, Malcolm will harvest venison from his land. The animals will have lived entirely free lives and will be humanely dispatched before being hung in his cold store. Nothing goes to waste.

Their love for the land is instinctive. Were it not for people like Sue and Malcolm, our beautiful county would not be such a beguiling place.

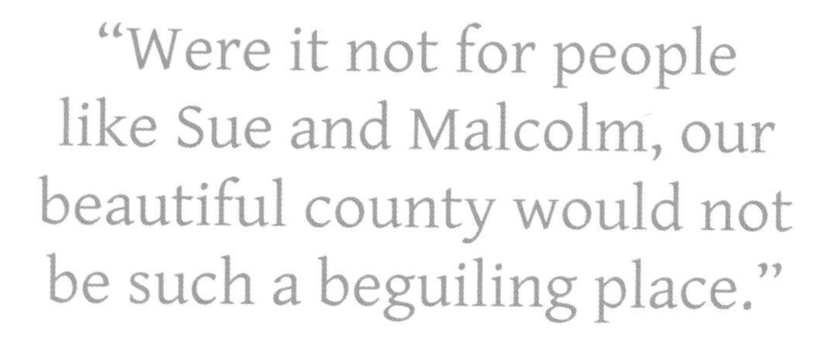

"Were it not for people like Sue and Malcolm, our beautiful county would not be such a beguiling place."

Pan-fried scallops, Bloody Mary jelly, black olive purée, gazpacho and parmesan crisp

SERVES 6

18 large hand-dived scallops
50ml rapeseed oil
50g unsalted butter

Bloody Mary jelly
300ml tomato juice
100ml vodka
6 splashes of Worcestershire sauce
Dash of Tabasco
1 lemon, juice only
Salt and pepper
2 leaves gelatine
9 × 50ml moulds

Gazpacho
1 red pepper, chopped and deseeded
1 small red onion
1 garlic clove
¼ cucumber, peeled, seeded and chopped
142ml extra virgin olive oil
250ml tomato juice
1 tbsp white-wine vinegar
1 tbsp sherry
Salt and pepper

Black olive purée
125g black olives
25g marinated anchovies
½ clove garlic
20g capers
Olive oil to bind
Salt and pepper

Parmesan crisps
Grated parmesan – around 6 tbsp, enough to spread evenly to make six crisps using a 5cm pastry cutter as a template

To garnish
Celery leaves (or parsley)

Remove the scallops from their shells, discarding the skirt and orange roe. Wash in cold water and drain on a clean towel. Place in the fridge to set firm. Do not leave the scallops in the water – they are like sponges and will absorb excess moisture. You will have to pay a lot more for hand-dived scallops, as opposed to dredged ones. Dredged scallops tend to be full of sand, and once that is embedded in the flesh it is hard to get out.

Bloody Mary jelly. Soak the gelatine in cold water until soft. Warm the tomato juice, remove from the heat, add the gelatine and pass through a fine sieve. Add vodka, Worcestershire sauce, Tabasco, lemon juice, salt and pepper. Pour into the moulds and set in the fridge overnight.

Gazpacho. Place all the vegetables and tomato juice in a blender and process until smooth. Pass through a fine sieve. Pour back into the blender/liquidiser, turn the machine and slowly pour in the olive oil, and finally add the sherry, vinegar, salt and pepper. Pass through a fine sieve again and store in the fridge until needed.

Black olive purée. Put all of the ingredients into a food processor and blend until smooth. You want to be able to mould the purée between two spoons – add a little olive oil if needed.

Parmesan crisps. On a non-stick baking mat lay out six circles of parmesan, evenly spread, using a 5cm pastry cutter as a pattern. Make sure the mat is covered but not too thickly. You want the result to be thin and crisp. Bake at 180C for about six minutes or until golden. Remove from the oven and cool slightly until you can slide a palette knife or spatula beneath. Lift off the tray – before they go cold – and shape over a rolling pin. If they get too cold, rewarm them in the oven, then shape.

Celery leaves. Deep fry as a garnish.

Serving. Turn a jelly out into the middle of the plate. Place three quenelles of black olive purée around the outside.

Season the scallops, heat a non-stick pan with rapeseed oil and cook the scallops on a medium heat for about a minute, until golden. Turn over, add butter and cook for another minute so that both top and bottom are golden. Drain on kitchen paper and squeeze lemon juice over to season.

Place a scallop alongside each quenelle, drizzle with gazpacho, garnish with deep-fried celery leaves and lean a parmesan crisp on the side of the jelly.

Chilled garden-pea mousse, tempura of sole, cress, pea shoots and tartare dressing

SERVES 6

Pea mousse
300ml double cream
100ml milk
200g frozen peas
Salt and pepper
2 leaves gelatine
3 tsp white-wine vinegar

Sole
6 lemon sole fillets
100g tempura flour – for a gluten-free version use 70g gluten-free plain flour and 30g gluten-free self-raising flour
180ml light beer or lager

Tartare dressing
2 egg yolks
1 tsp mustard
1 tsp white-wine vinegar
300ml rapeseed oil
1 tbsp capers, roughly chopped
2 gherkins, finely diced
1 tsp parsley, chopped

Pea mousse. Soak the gelatine leaves in cold water. Bring the cream and milk to a boil, add the frozen peas and cook for two minutes. Take off the heat and add the gelatine. When dissolved, liquidise until smooth. Pass through a fine sieve.

Add vinegar, salt and pepper. Pour into six bowls and set in the fridge. This can be done the day before.

Sole. Cut each sole fillets into two. Mix the flour with the beer (do not overmix, and if using a gluten-free version you might require a little more liquid, as the flour absorbs more moisture). Pass the sole through the batter and deep fry at 190C until golden and crisp. Drain on kitchen paper.

Tartare dressing. Mix the yolks, mustard and vinegar. Add oil, a little at a time, whisking all the while until it is all incorporated. Check for seasoning. Add capers, gherkins and parsley. Check for consistency, adjusting with a little warm water if it is too thick.

Serving. Bring the bowls of mousse from the fridge and wipe the edges of the plates to remove any moisture. Dress a little salad garnish with olive oil and arrange in a neat pile on top of the mousse, in the middle. Then lay deep-fried sole over the top and drizzle with dressing.

Bayleaf panna cotta, char-grilled new potatoes, ham knuckle, mustard and onion rings

SERVES 6

Panna cotta
200ml double cream
100ml milk
10 dried bayleaves, crushed
1 leaf gelatine
Salt and pepper

Ham knuckle
1 ham knuckle
1 small onion, peeled and chopped
1 small carrot, peeled and chopped
1 stick celery, chopped
½ leek, washed and chopped
2 bayleaves
1 sprig thyme
Cold water/chicken stock, enough to cover the knuckle

Potatoes
6 new potatoes

Mustard dressing
2 egg yolks
1 tsp English mustard
1 tsp white-wine vinegar
300ml rapeseed oil
Salt and pepper
1 tbsp mustard seeds

Onion rings
18 thin slices of onion, cut from near the middle
100ml milk
100g strong flour
1 tsp paprika

Panna cotta. Soak the gelatine in cold water until soft. Bring the milk, cream and bayleaves to the boil in a pan and simmer gently for two minutes. Add the gelatine and, when it has dissolved, pass through a fine sieve. Fill six moulds and chill in the fridge. This can be done a day in advance, which gives them plenty of time to set firm.

Ham knuckle. Put the knuckle into a pan with all of the other ingredients. Bring to a boil, turn down and simmer gently for about two-and-a-half hours or until the knuckle is tender. When cooked, take the pan off the heat and allow the knuckle to cool in the liquid. Again this can be done the day before you need it. When cold, remove and reserve the liquid in case it is needed.

Potatoes. Cook the potatoes in simmering salted water until cooked, and allow to cool in the water. Take this slow cooling into consideration, so do not overcook. When cold, slice each potato into three, and chargrill on each side. If you don't have a chargrill just warm gently.

Mustard dressing. Whisk the egg yolks, mustard and vinegar together. Slowly add the oil, a little at a time, whisking all the time until combined. Season. Mix in the mustard seeds. You may need to add liquid to obtain a drizzling consistency – if so use reserved ham stock.

Onion rings. Mix the paprika into the flour. Pass the onions rings through the milk and then coat in the flour. Deep fry at 190C until golden. Drain on kitchen paper.

Serving. Pick the ham knuckle into 18 pieces, cover with a little dressing and warm slightly in a pan on a low heat.

Turn each panna cotta out into the middle of a plate. Put three slices of potatoes around, and three pieces of ham. Drizzle with dressing and garnish with pea shoots (or something similar) and three onion rings.

Chilled horseradish mousse, smoked mackerel, beetroot and blood orange

SERVES 6

2 smoked mackerel fillets
18 segments blood orange

Mousse
150ml double cream
75ml milk
2 tbsp horseradish relish
1 leaf gelatine
Salt and pepper

Beetroots and dressing
6 medium-sized beetroots (see method)
2 egg yolks
1 tsp English mustard
1 tsp white-wine vinegar
300ml rapeseed oil

Mousse. Soak the gelatine in cold water until soft. Bring the cream, milk and horseradish to the boil in a pan, season with salt and pepper. Remove from the heat and add gelatine to the warm liquid. When dissolved pass through a fine sieve. Fill six moulds and chill in the fridge. This can be done the day before they are needed.

Smoked mackerel. If you have a smoker you can smoke your own or you can buy ready-smoked from your fishmonger. Our fishmongers smoke their own and it is the best I have ever tasted. Remove the skin and break into 18 pieces.

Beetroot. The day before you need them, wash the beetroots thoroughly and cook in salted water until tender. Take off the heat. When cool, peel them and put back into the liquid to cool completely. Leave overnight.

Take the beetroots and trim to make them square. Cut into 5mm dice. Put beetroots aside and keep the trimmings for the dressing.

Whisk the egg yolks, vinegar and mustard together. Slowly add the oil, little by little, whisking all the time. Keep those ingredients at room temperature, as it will help them all mix together. Place in a small food processor with the beetroot trimmings. Blend until smooth. Check seasoning, and if a little too thick to drizzle add a little beetroot water.

Serving. On each plate put three teaspoons of natural yoghurt and drag the spoon through to create ‘teardrops’. Turn the panna cotta out into the middle of the plate.

Arrange diced beetroot, orange segments and warm mackerel around the edge of the plate and drizzle with dressing. Garnish with micro-herbs.

Twice-baked goat's cheese and garlic soufflé

MAKES 12–15

42g butter
42g flour
1 whole bulb garlic
340g goat's cheese, cut up small
5 egg yolks
6 egg whites
284ml milk
White breadcrumbs

Apple sauce
2 apples, peeled, cored and sliced – I use Braeburns
10g butter
1 tsp lemon juice

Celeriac salad
2 egg yolks
1 tsp mustard
1 tsp white-wine vinegar
300ml rapeseed oil
1 medium celeriac
1 apple
1 tsp chopped chives

Apple dressing
30g honey
30ml water
30ml cider vinegar
250ml apple juice
50ml cider
15ml olive oil

Pickled walnuts – shop-bought ones are fine

The soufflé mix makes between 12 and 15, though the purée and accompaniments serve between four and six, depending on whether you are serving the dish as a starter or a main. The remaining soufflés can be frozen and used at a later date.

Roast the whole bulb of garlic on a bed of salt. The salt will penetrate during cooking. Don't worry if the outer skins go dry and brown. Roast in an oven at 180C for about 20 minutes. When cooked take out and cut the bottom off. Squeeze out six cloves.

In a thick-bottomed pan, melt the butter, add the flour and cook out for a couple of minutes on a low heat. Add the milk a little at a time, whisking thoroughly until you have added all the milk. This will look like a white sauce, béchamel.

Add the garlic. Cook on a low heat for five minutes. Do not leave, otherwise it will stick. Add the egg yolks and cook for about five minutes.

Take off the heat. Add the goat's cheese and allow to melt. When combined, transfer to a large bowl. Cover with cling film, keep warm and do not allow a skin to form.

Prepare your soufflé moulds by buttering moulds/ramekins. Fill the first one with white breadcrumbs, tip in to the next mould and continue for all. (You could use ground walnuts instead of breadcrumbs.)

Whisk the egg whites to soft peaks, avoiding overwhisking which causes a grainy textured soufflé. Mix one third into your cheese mix. Now gently fold in the remaining whites.

Fill your ramekins to about two-thirds full and place in a water bath. Cover with buttered tin foil/greaseproof and put into a preheated oven for 20 minutes at 125C. We just want them to set, not expand.

When cooked and set, sponge-like, remove from the oven and allow to cool. When cold turn out onto a tray. Place in the fridge covered with cling film. I always make mine the day before. They will also freeze really well in an airtight container.

Apple sauce. Place the ingredients in a pan and cook on a low heat until soft. You may need to add a little water/apple juice to get it started. Once cooked blend in a food processor until smooth. Set aside.

Celeriac salad. Make mayonnaise by whisking the egg yolks, vinegar and mustard together. Slowly add the oil a little at a time until combined. Season with salt and pepper. Peel the celeriac and cut into thin matchstick strips, by hand or using a mandolin.

Blanch the celeriac in hot water and refresh in cold water. This makes it limp. Dry between kitchen paper. When dry add into the mayonnaise.

Peel the apple, slice and shred to a similar size to the celeriac. I find this easier to do by hand. Mix with the celeriac and add the chopped chives.

Apple dressing. Put the sugar and water in a heavy-bottomed pan and heat gently on a low heat until the sugar has dissolved. Turn up the heat and cook until the sugar starts to turn a caramel colour. Add the cider vinegar and reduce to a syrup. Add apple juice and cider and simmer until reduced to a syrup. Take off the heat and whisk in the oil.

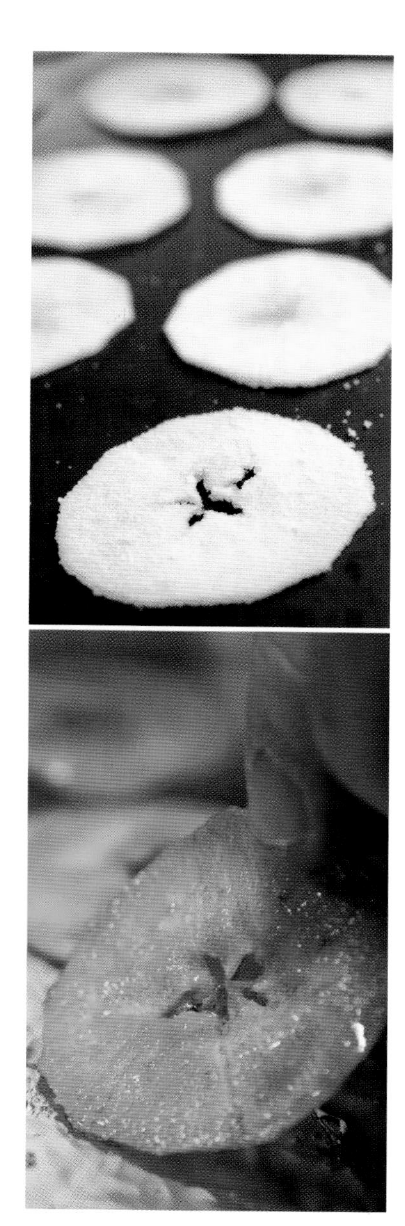

Serving. Put the soufflés on a non-stick baking mat or non-stick baking tray. Spoon a tablespoon of double cream over each soufflé and some grated cheddar or other cheese. Dress your plates before cooking the soufflés; once they come out of the oven they must be served straight away.

Place three teaspoons of apple sauce onto your plate and drag a spoon through each one to create 'teardrops'. Place some celeriac onto the middle of each plate. Slice pickled walnuts and place three slices around the plate. Decorate the plate with either mustard and cress or micro-herbs around the plate. Put the soufflés in a hot oven preheated to 200C and cook until the cheese is golden and the soufflés have risen. It will take eight to ten minutes. Remove from the tray and put a soufflé on top of each plate.

Go! Go! Go!

I'm not the only man who is passionate about local produce. Father-and-son team Phillip and Ian Warren are also great advocates for Devon's immaculate larder.

I've worked with them for more than a decade and am proud of the association.

Initially, they ran a small butcher's shop in the centre of Launceston. But in recent times they've moved to bigger premises on the edge of town, where they have a unit for hanging and cutting meat.

The Warrens' shop is a work of art. The counter is stocked with the best of local produce. Flavoursome fillets and succulent steaks compete for space with lesser-used cuts, such as shin, tail and offal. Everything is presented so beautifully that it's no wonder they have queues down the street at the busiest times of year.

I'm a great believer in supporting the local food economy and doing all that we can to help our local farmers. The Warrens share those beliefs and work closely with people who are the backbone of our region's economy.

They slaughter livestock humanely and show the same care and affection for those animals after they've been dispatched.

Occasionally, I go to their meat rooms to see how they're doing things. I am always reassured that they are upholding the highest standards.

They can tell me where every animal has come from and exactly how long it's been with them, down to the last minute. That means I can pass that information on to my customers, providing guarantees on quality. I'm able to name the farm that raised a particular animal. It helps to build confidence and trust in the local foodchain.

The Warrens provide a bespoke operation. I favour beef, for instance, that has been hung for 28 days – though they would hang it for twice that length of time if I asked them to. They invest in the best equipment and use intelligent methods.

In one of their refrigeration rooms, they pile large blocks of salted ice on a big metal rack. The blocks help to extract moisture from the atmosphere, intensifying the flavour of the meat and giving the fat an almost sweet, buttery flavour.

The Warrens provide the link from farm to fork, ensuring that animals are well cared for and that meat is diligently prepared. Like me, they are passionate about providing the best welfare and highest quality. And that means I can have confidence and trust in the dishes that I deliver to my customers.

“They can tell me where every animal has come from and exactly how long it’s been with them, down to the last minute.”

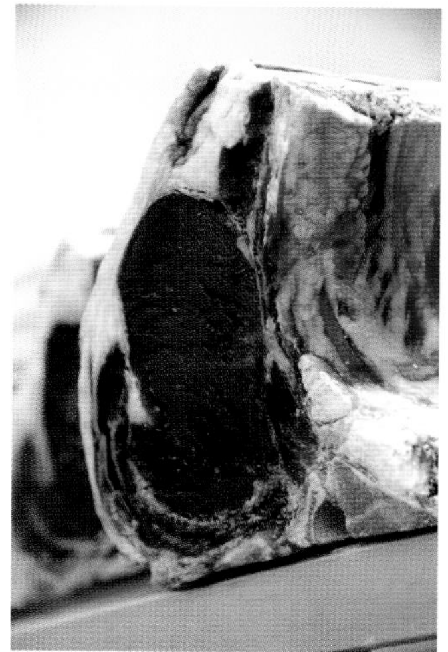

Breast of guinea fowl, beer-battered corned beef, truffled cabbage, almond croquette potatoes and beetroot

SERVES 4

4 breasts of guinea fowl
200g corned beef
100g tempura flour
small bottle light beer
300g savoy cabbage
1 tsp truffle peelings
500g potatoes
75g butter
100g ground almonds
100g breadcrumbs
500g beetroot – keep some for garnish
1000ml beef stock

Garnish
Pan-fried seasonal vegetables and beetroot

Croquette potatoes. Cook potatoes in boiling salted water. Drain when cooked, and leave to dry. Mash and mix in butter. When cool enough, roll into walnut-sized balls. Pass through seasoned flour and then eggwash and finally through a mix of the ground almonds and breadcrumbs. Fry croquettes at the same time as the fritters.

Beetroot sauce. Cook beetroot in boiling salted water, and when tender leave to cool in the water. Reduce the beef stock by half and put into liquidiser with peeled beetroot. Liquidise, then pass through a fine sieve.

Cabbage. Pick the leaves off the stalks and chop into small pieces. Cook in boiling salted water. When cooked place into iced cold water to refresh. Warm the cabbage in a little butter with some truffle peelings just as you are about to serve.

Corned beef fritters. Dice the corned beef into bite-sized chunks. Mix the tempura flour very lightly with the beer. Toss the corned beef into batter and deep fry at 180C at the last minute. (If you can't get tempura flour you can use self-raising flour.)

Guinea fowl. Seal the breast all over and cook in oven for five or six minutes, then leave to rest. Assemble as shown.

Roasted chump of lamb, haggis ravioli, swede purée, confit shallots and garlic, and carrot juices

SERVES 6

Lamb chump
6 × 225g chumps of lamb
50ml rapeseed oil
25g unsalted butter

Haggis ravioli
1 batch of ravioli dough (page 66)
110g haggis
1 egg, beaten

Swede purée
300g swede, peeled and diced
125ml double cream
100ml milk
50g unsalted butter

Confit shallots and garlic
18 shallots, peeled
18 cloves of garlic, peeled
100ml duck fat
2 bay leaves
2 sprigs of thyme

Carrot juices
300g carrots, peeled and chopped
500ml white chicken stock
1 tsp ground cumin
200ml rapeseed oil

Heat the rapeseed oil and butter in a non-stick pan, season the lamb and put into the pan, fat-side down. Cook until golden. Turnover and seal the meat side. Do not allow to crisp or burn. Put into an ovenproof dish, fat-side down and cook at 180C for approximately 12 minutes. Remove from the oven and rest.

Haggis ravioli. Roll out your pasta to the desired thickness. You need two sheets. Brush with egg wash. Divide the haggis into six equal balls. Place them onto one of your sheets of dough, leaving enough room to cut around each ball with a cutter. Place the other sheet of dough on top, encasing the haggis.

Gently press the dough around the haggis, removing all the air as you go and sealing top and bottom sheets of pasta together. Cut out each ravioli with a cutter.

Cook for 90 seconds in a pan of boiling salted water. Remove and refresh in ice-cold water. When cold take out and drain on a cloth. Keep in the fridge until service.

Swede purée. Put all of the ingredients into a suitable pan and bring to the boil. Turn down the heat and simmer until the swede is tender. Place in a small food processor and blend until smooth. Season to taste and keep warm.

Confit shallots and garlic. Put the shallots and garlic into a pan of boiling salted water and blanch for a minute. Refresh in ice-cold water. Place on a sheet of tin foil with the duck fat, bay leaf and thyme. Fold the foil, creating a tightly sealed parcel. Cook in a preheated oven at 180C for 25 minutes. Remove from the oven and cool.

Carrot juices. In a heavy-based pan add the carrots, stock and cumin. Bring to the boil, turn the heat down and simmer until soft. Liquidise until smooth, then pass through a fine sieve. Return to the liquidiser, turn on and slowly add the oil to emulsify. Check seasoning.

Serving. In a non-stick frying pan warm the lamb through with the shallots and garlic. The ravioli needs to go back into a pan of boiling salted water for one-and-a-half to two minutes. Warm the swede purée in a small pan. Place a spoon of purée on your plate and drag a spoon through it to resemble a teardrop.

Place the shallots and garlic around the outside of the plate and put some buttered cabbage into the centre. Lay your lamb on top of that, with the ravioli on top of the lamb.

Drizzle with carrot juices.

Duck confit

SERVES 6

6 duck legs
200g coarse sea salt
100g ground black pepper
1 head garlic, separated into cloves
12 sprigs of thyme
3 dried bayleaves, crumbled
1kg duck fat

Confit is one of our most popular dishes, yet a surprisingly small number of people know how to do it. This recipe, therefore, is intended to illustrate the confit method, which you can use to cook duck legs, pork belly or many other cuts of meat and game. We serve this particular dish with sauté potatoes and a green salad, but you could serve it with a tomato and morel salad, puy lentils or a variety of other accompaniments.

Rub the duck legs with the sea salt, black pepper, bayleaves, garlic and thyme. Place them into a suitable dish, cover with cling film and leave to marinate in the fridge for 24 hours.

Preheat the oven to 150C. Heat the duck fat in a heavy-bottomed ovenproof pan or casserole dish. When the duck fat has melted, remove the marinade from the duck legs and completely submerge them in the fat.

Transfer the dish to the oven and cook for three-and-a-half to four hours, or until the meat is very tender and the fat is completely rendered. Remove the pan from the oven and allow the legs to cool in the duck fat. If you leave them in the fat they can be stored in the fridge for up to a month. I make them in batches of 24 legs at a time and then vac-pac them individually, freezing until I want them.

When you want to reheat, scrape off as much fat as you can. Place in a non-stick roasting tray, skin-side up and reheat in the oven for about 30 minutes or until the skin is crisp.

Serve immediately.

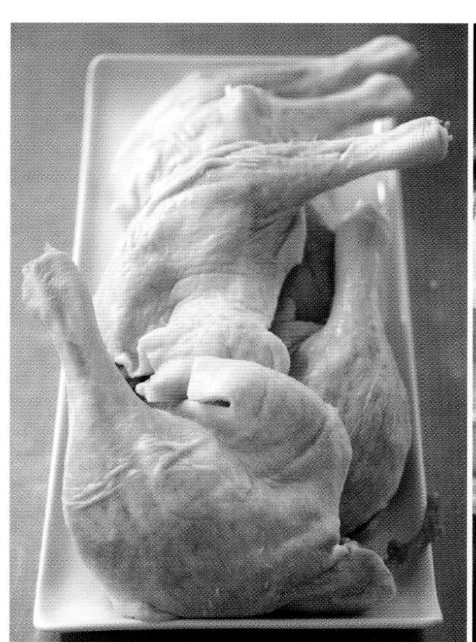

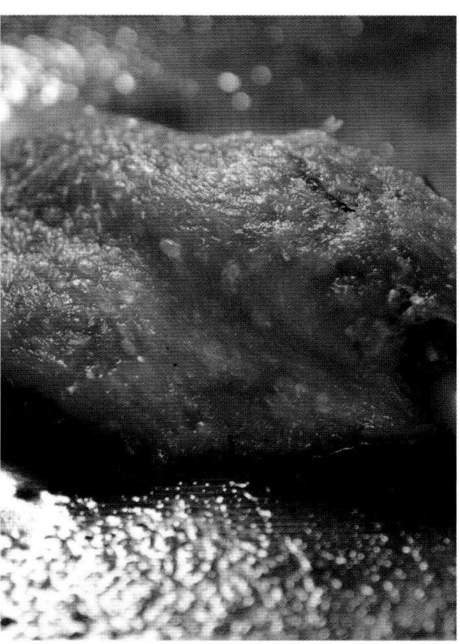

Crispy belly of pork

SERVES 6

1 medium onion, sliced
2 bayleaves
1 sprig of thyme
2kg piece of belly pork, skin removed for crackling, rib bones removed for sauce
1 garlic head (optional)
1 carrot, peeled and cut into 1cm dice
2 sticks of celery, cut into 1cm dice
3000ml duck fat – if you think this will be too rich, use either ham or chicken stock

Butternut squash purée
1kg butternut squash
50ml rapeseed oil
200ml milk
150ml double cream
50ml sesame oil

Apple and cumin compôte
4 apples, peeled, cored and cut into small dice. Put straight into lemon-juice water, to avoid browning
1 onion, peeled and finely diced
1 level tbsp cumin
300ml apple juice
1 tbsp honey
50ml white-wine vinegar

Crackling
Use the skin from the belly, score and rub in rapeseed oil and salt.

Pork sauce
50ml rapeseed oil
Bones from the belly, chopped small
2 shallots, finely diced
1 garlic clove, finely sliced
1 carrot, peeled and chopped small
1 sprig thyme
1 bayleaf
4 cloves, crushed
25g unsalted butter
1 tbsp honey
300ml cider
1000ml brown stock

Sage gnocchi
300g potatoes
60g plain flour
40g hard cheddar cheese, finely grated
1 tbsp rapeseed oil
Salt and pepper
10 sage leaves, finely chopped

Belly pork. Spread the onion, bayleaf, thyme, garlic, carrots and celery in a large-enough pan with two tablespoons of rapeseed oil. Place a lid on and sweat the vegetables. Stir often and check they aren't burning.

Put the pork in, cover with duck fat or stock, and bring up to 96C. Cover with a lid or foil and place in a preheated oven and cook for three-and-a-half to four hours at 160C, or until tender. Allow it to cool in the duck fat or stock. When cold, remove the pork and wrap tightly in cling film and refrigerate overnight. Next day trim the meat to give a neat shape. Keep the trimmings and use them in the sauce. Cut the pork into six equal pieces.

Gnocchi. Boil the potatoes in salted water. When cooked, drain and return to the pan and cover with a tea towel and lid. Place back on a low heat and keep shaking the pan so that the potatoes are really dry.

When dry, either rice or mash them.

Add the flour, grated cheddar, rapeseed oil and chopped sage. Bring it all together to form a dough, roll into long sausage shapes and cut into 2–3cm lengths. Bring a large pan of water to the boil and cook the gnocchi until they float to the surface. It should take about a minute. Do not cook too many together – it's best to cook in batches. Remove with a slotted spoon and drain. Repeat until all the dough is cooked. Heat a frying pan until hot and add a tablespoon of oil. Add the gnocchi and fry until golden brown. Set aside.

Pork sauce. Heat the rapeseed oil, add the pork ribs and trimmings. Cook until browned. Add the vegetables and herbs, cover with a lid and sweat until cooked. Remove the lid, add the honey and allow to caramelise, add the cider and reduce to concentrate all the flavours. Add the stock and reduce until about 200ml is left. Pass through a sieve.

Squash purée. Quarter the squash, remove any seeds and place onto a baking tray. Drizzle with a little oil, add salt and pepper, and cover with tin foil. Roast in the oven at 200C until the flesh is soft and tender.

Remove from the oven and scrape all the flesh from the skin. Bring the cream and milk to the boil, pour into a small food processor with the squash flesh and blend until smooth. Blend in the sesame oil. The hotter you can keep everything, the more smoothly it will blend. Keep warm.

Crackling. Cut the pork skin into thin strips and cook sandwiched between two baking sheets with a weight on the top tray. Cook at 180C for about 10 minutes. Make sure

you keep an eye on it and drain off any excess fat. (If too much fat escapes and you are using a gas oven, there could be the possibility of fat going into the gas burners and causing a fire.) When cooked, remove from the tray and allow to cool on a rack.

Compôte. Put onion, cumin and a tablespoon of rapeseed oil into a saucepan and sweat until the onion is soft. Add the honey and white-wine vinegar, and reduce to a syrup. Add the apple juice and reduce again to a thick syrup consistency. Add the diced apple and allow to cook until the fruit is soft. Remove from the heat and keep warm.

Serving. To finish the pork, heat 50ml of oil in a large cast-iron or non-stick pan. When hot, place the pork in skin-side down. Turn the heat down low, and cook until the skin is crisp. Turn it over at any time if you think it's going too fast. Also turn the meat onto its sides. Cook the pork until it's heated all the way through.

Present in a way that you like, or as illustrated.

Rack of lamb, braised shoulder, crisp sweetbreads, garlic purée, wilted wild garlic and kidney gravy

SERVES 6

1 rack of lamb with six bones, French-trimmed (ask your butcher to do this for you)
1 shoulder of lamb, boned and rolled (again, ask your butcher to do this)
6 kidneys, cut in half to remove poles

For the sweetbreads
6 lamb sweetbreads
15g seasoned flour
1 tbsp rapeseed oil
1 tsp ground cumin

For garlic purée
4 heads of garlic
50ml rapeseed oil
150ml double cream
50ml milk

For wilted garlic
40g unsalted butter
150g wild garlic leaves

For lamb sauce
50ml rapeseed oil
2 shallots, finely chopped
2 sprigs thyme
1 small carrot, peeled and finely chopped
1 bayleaf
1 sprig rosemary
All the bones from the lamb – ask the butcher to keep them for you, chopped small
1000ml brown stock

Prepare your shoulder of lamb 24 hours in advance. Remove the bone, thick fat and sinew. Cut it in half lengthways. If you use the whole shoulder boned and rolled it makes the overall finished diameter too large.

Once cut in half season with salt and pepper, brush with English mustard and sprinkle with cumin and chopped rosemary. Roll tightly in cling film to form a cylinder. Refrigerate for an hour. Take out, remove cling film and tie with string.

Heat the oil and butter in a pan and brown the lamb all over. Remove the lamb, add chopped vegetables to the pan and cook until golden. Add herbs and stock, bring to a boil and add the shoulder. Cover with a lid and place in to the oven 140C and cook until the meat is tender. The slower it cooks the better: three to four hours.

Allow it to cool just enough so that you can handle it, then wrap in cling film into a cylinder. That helps retain the moisture and prevents dryness. Refrigerate overnight, to set the shape.

Strain the sauce through a fine sieve and reduce. Refrigerate overnight.

After the lamb has been in the fridge overnight, cut through the cling film into 115g pieces. Reheat the sauce, and add the lamb; do not let the temperature rise above 83C. Heat for 15 minutes.

Sweetbreads. Blanch the sweetbreads in boiling water for three to four minutes. Drain and refresh in cold water. Remove the outer membrane, pass through cumin-infused seasoned flour. Heat the oil and cook for four or five minutes, turning often until crispy. Drain on kitchen paper.

Lamb sauce. Heat the oil in a saucepan, add the lamb bones, brown but do not burn. Add all of the other ingredients except the stock. Place a lid on the pan and turn the heat down low. Sweat until the vegetables start to soften. Add the stock and simmer for 30 minutes. Pass through a fine sieve. Reduce to about 200ml and adjust seasoning.

Rack of lamb. Season the rack with salt and pepper. Heat about 50ml of rapeseed oil, add 25g unsalted butter and sizzle, then brown the lamb, sealing it. Place in the oven at 180C for eight to ten minutes. Take out and allow to rest for five minutes. Keep warm.

Garlic purée. Separate the garlic cloves but do not peel. Blanch in boiling salted water for 1 minute, refresh in cold water. Repeat twice. Toss them in rapeseed oil and place in tightly sealed tin foil, so as to retain the steam. Cook for about 20 minutes or until garlic is soft. Remove from the foil and remove garlic skins. Put the garlic, double cream and milk into a small pan and boil. Season and blend in a small blender until smooth.

Wilted wild garlic. Heat the butter in a frying pan. Wash the wild garlic in cold water and drain, leaving slightly damp. Add to the butter and keep turning the garlic over and over to evenly distribute the heat. Cook over a medium heat until the leaves are tender. Drain and season. Keep warm.

Assemble as shown.

Pan-fried beef fillet, truffle croquette potatoes, parsnip purée, beetroots and baby onions

SERVES 6

6 × 225g beef fillet steaks
25ml rapeseed oil
25g unsalted butter

Beef sauce
50ml rapeseed oil
100g smoked bacon trimmings
1 small onion, peeled and chopped
1 small carrot, peeled and chopped
6 button mushrooms, washed and sliced
2 sprigs of thyme, leaves only
200ml red wine
200ml Madeira
1000ml brown stock

Truffled croquette potatoes
300g potatoes, peeled
50g unsalted butter
100g truffle peelings, chopped
Seasoned flour
Beaten egg
White breadcrumbs

Parsnip purée
See page 80

Beetroot and baby onions
18 baby onions, peeled
18 baby beetroots
25ml duck fat
2 sprigs of thyme, leaves only
Zest of 1 orange

Heat the oil in a non-stick pan, add butter and when it starts to foam add the seasoned beef fillet. Seal all over and keep turning to cook evenly. Put into an ovenproof dish into a preheated oven at 200C for five to eight minutes, depending on how rare you like it. Remove and rest for five minutes.

Beef sauce. Heat the oil in a heavy-bottomed pan, add chopped bacon and fry until golden. Remove and place in a bowl.

Turn the gas down, put in the vegetables and thyme, put a lid on the pan and sweat. When the vegetables are cooked add the red wine and Madeira then reduce by two thirds. Add the brown stock, simmer and reduce until you have 200ml left. Pass through a fine sieve into a clean pan and keep warm.

Truffled croquette potatoes. Cook the potatoes in salted boiling water until soft. Drain and make sure they are dry. Mash with a hand-masher then mix in the butter, salt and pepper and truffles. You can either roll them out into balls or a classic cylindrical shape. Place on a tray covered with cling film and refrigerate. When cold pass through seasoned flour, beaten egg and breadcrumbs. Deep fry at 180C until golden.

Parsnip purée. Follow the instructions on page 80.

Beetroots and baby onions. Wash the beetroots and trim the tops, leaving a little stalk. Put into a bowl with the baby onions, thyme, orange zest and duck fat. Put onto tin foil and fold into a tight parcel. Place onto a baking sheet and cook at 180C for 20 minutes until tender. Remove and when cool enough to handle peel the beetroots.

Serving. Toss the beetroots and onions in a little butter and deep-fry the potato croquettes. Place three spoons of parsnip purée on the plate and draw a spoon through to create a teardrop. Around the outside of the plate alternatively place beetroots, baby onions and croquettes. Place a little buttered spinach into the centre of the plate and top with the steaks and finish with a drizzle of sauce.

"I'm living the dream," is the catchphrase of my egg supplier, Darren. On wild and wet mornings, it sounds like a joke. But he means every last word.

Darren and his wife, Joy, moved to Devon from Derbyshire and have been farming here since around 2005. He has 12,000 chickens which roam freely on a farm just 10 minutes away from us.

He's devoted to his birds, tending them in all weathers and making sure they are happy and healthy. The quality of their eggs is testament to his high standards of care. Vivid golden yolks with an intense flavour are delivered to our doorstep each week.

His farm is set in the rolling countryside in an isolated rural location. His birds greedily feast on corn that he scatters on the ground, making the most of their feed.

He, like many others, is doing it for love of it.

"I had a very different life before I moved to Devon," he says. "But we couldn't be happier than we are now. We love the birds and we give them a good life. We also get on really well with our customers. Quality is important to us and we do everything that we can to make sure we deliver the best possible eggs to our customers."

Darren walks it like he talks it. When he's not out tending the birds, he's on the high seas in his kayak. Like many local producers, he works formidably hard but then tries to make the best of the beautiful countryside in which we live.

"Living the dream" – he's not joking.

Pasta

MAKES 1 BATCH

300g "00" flour
8 egg yolks
1 tbsp olive oil
Salt and pepper

Place the flour and a pinch of salt in a food processor. Mix the eggs and olive oil together. Turn on the machine and pour the eggs in. Stop the machine as soon as it comes together.

Tip out onto a lightly floured surface. If the dough is a little dry add a little more egg, and if too wet add a little more flour.

Knead for five minutes until you have a smooth dough. Wrap in cling film and put into the fridge for a least 30 minutes.

Use your pasta machine to roll out as thinly as possible and then cut into the required shape.

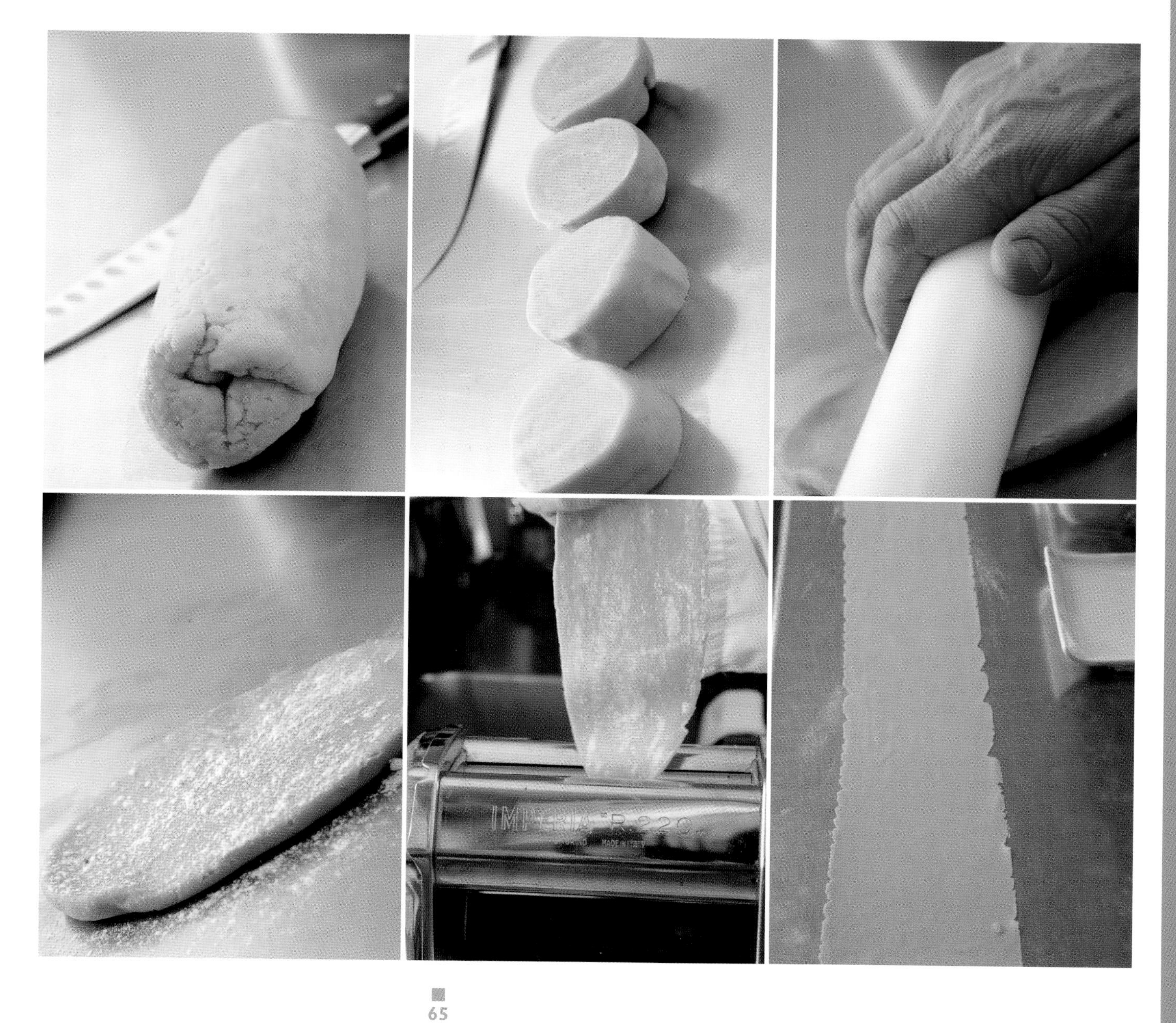

IMPERIA R.220

Tortellini

Using a pasta machine roll out pasta dough on the finest setting. Cut 12 circles of 6–7cm diameter, and place a small amount of the filling of your choice into the centre of your first disc.

Brush the edge with a little beaten egg and fold the top half over so you have a semi-circle. Make sure you get all of the air out.

When you press the edges together, curl the semi-circle around your finger, joining the two corners together, so you get the classic tortellini shape. Repeat this process for all 12.

Blanch in a large pan of boiling salted water for two minutes. Refresh in cold water and place on a cloth and cover with cling film for later.

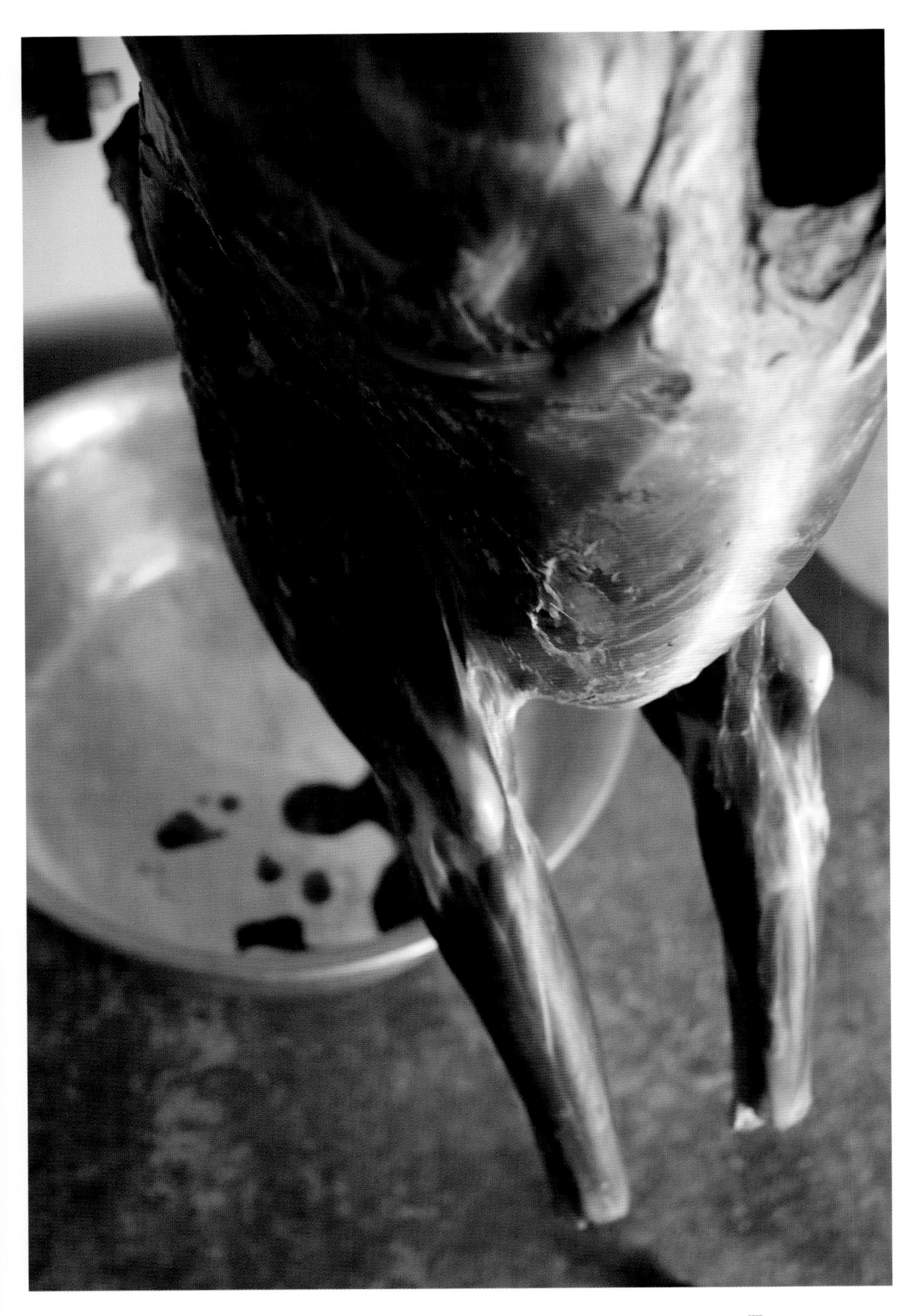

Devon teems with wildlife and much of it is in full view. We see deer canter across our lawns, on their way to some nearby wood. Owls nest in the local trees. There are myriad finches and tits. Wild ducks fly in for short spells of the year and families of woodpeckers make their home just a stone's throw from our home. Most of the wildlife is rightly protected. Like our guests, Liz and I marvel at the creatures. Watching them play out their lives is a remarkably tranquil and life-affirming pursuit.

Of course, the game season brings nature's bounty to our table during autumn and winter. It passes all too quickly and we try to make the most of robust, flavoursome dishes when we can.

We live in a rural area and the age-old tradition of bagging a rabbit for the pot endures. Many people who live nearby harvest game during the season; roasting, slow-cooking, braising and stewing their catch.

One of the beauties of being so immersed in the countryside is that we observe at first hand the full and rewarding lives that such creatures lead.

When the time comes, they are humanely dispatched, which helps to maintain the delicate balance of our countryside.

During the chilly months, when frost is on the ground, we can enjoy the earthy, rich flavours of venison, pheasant, partridge and other seasonal delights.

Many people who live nearby harvest game during the season; roasting, slow-cooking, braising and stewing their catch.

Peppercorn-and-juniper-crusted roe deer, celeriac, pickled pears, truffles and sugared walnuts

SERVES 6

6 × 150g venison steaks from the saddle
1 tbsp crushed black peppercorns
1 tbsp crushed juniper berries
50ml rapeseed oil
25g unsalted butter

Celeriac purée
300g celeriac, peeled and diced small
125ml double cream
150ml milk
75g unsalted butter

Pickled pears
3 pears, peeled, halved and core removed with a Parisian scoop
400g light soft brown sugar
400ml red-wine vinegar
Zest of 1 lemon
Zest of 1 orange
5 cloves
1 vanilla pod
1 cinnamon stick
5 coriander seeds
15g fresh ginger root
3 crushed cardamom pods
2 bayleaves
1 tsp mixed spice

Sugared walnuts
18 halves of walnut
Caster sugar
1 tbsp walnut oil

Sauce for venison
50ml rapeseed oil
Venison bones, chopped up small
2 shallots, sliced
2 sprigs of thyme
1 small carrot, peeled and chopped small
6 mushrooms, sliced
100ml Madeira
1000ml brown stock
25ml truffle oil

Pears. Put all of the ingredients, except the pears, into a suitable pan and bring to the boil, stirring to dissolve the sugar. Reduce the heat and simmer for 20 minutes to maximise flavours. Take the poaching liquor off the stove and allow to cool.

Add the peeled and cored pears to the liquor and poach gently until tender. The cooking time will depend on the condition of the pears.

Once poached remove the pears and put into a suitable container. Reduce the liquor by half. Allow to cool and when almost cold pour over the pears. Store until needed and the colour of the pears will deepen.

Sauce for venison. Heat the oil in a heavy-bottomed pan, add the venison bones and brown all over. Turn the heat down, add the vegetables, put a lid on and sweat. Add the thyme and Madeira and reduce by half. Add the brown stock and simmer for 30 minutes. Pass through a fine sieve. Whisk in the truffle oil either by hand blender or electric stick blender.

Celeriac purée. Place the celeriac into a saucepan, add the milk and cream and bring to the boil. Turn down and simmer until the celeriac is soft. Put into a small food processor and blend until smooth. Season to taste and keep warm.

Venison. Season the venison with salt and pepper then coat in crushed peppercorns and juniper. Heat the oil and butter, seal the meat all over until golden. Transfer to a suitable dish and cook in the oven at 200C for about five minutes, depending on how rare you like it. Leave in a warm place for five minutes to rest.

Sugared walnuts. Place the walnuts in a pan of cold water, bring to the boil and simmer for about two minutes. Leave in the water and allow to cool until you can handle them. Peel as much of the skin off as you can: the skin imparts their bitter taste. Once they are peeled, pass them through the caster sugar and deep fry them at 200C until golden in colour but not too dark. Turn out onto a dish with the walnut oil and toss them in it. This will stop them sticking together when the sugar cools down.

Serving. You now have all of the components. Present using your own imagination, or as shown. Finish with sliced truffles and parsnip crisps.

Pan-fried breast of pheasant, groats pudding tortellini, morel mushrooms, kale and air-dried ham

SERVES 4

4 × pheasant breasts
25ml rapeseed oil
50g butter

Tortellini
1 batch pasta (see page 65)
1 groats pudding – if you can't get this use hog's pudding, or even your own filling
25ml rapeseed oil
1 small shallot, peeled and chopped
1 sprig of thyme, leaves only
25ml madeira
1 egg, beaten
200ml brown stock
100ml double cream

Morel mushrooms
15–18 morel mushrooms, depending on size
25ml rapeseed oil
10g butter

Air-dried ham
4 slices of air dried ham

Sauce for pheasant
25ml rapeseed oil
Pheasant bones
1 small red onion, peeled and chopped
1 small carrot, peeled and chopped
1 sprig of thyme
6 button mushrooms, washed and sliced
200ml madeira
1000ml brown stock

Heat a non-stick pan with the oil. Season the pheasant breasts with salt and pepper and seal in the hot oil. Add the butter and let it froth and sizzle. You just want to seal the breasts and get some colour on them, especially the skin, but be careful as they can split. Transfer to an ovenproof dish and cook for six to seven minutes at 180C. Take out and rest.

Tortellini. In a pan heat the rapeseed oil, add shallot and thyme and cook until the shallot is translucent but uncoloured. Add Madeira and reduce by half. Add stock and reduce by half. Add double cream and bring to the boil, then simmer until a sauce consistency is achieved. Take off the heat and add the groats pudding. Season and refrigerate to cool.

Make your tortellini following the method on page 67.

Morel mushrooms. Rinse the mushrooms under cold water to remove any dirt and pat dry using kitchen paper. Heat the oil and butter in a pan. When the butter starts to foam add the mushrooms and cook on a moderate heat for two or three minutes, depending on the size. Shake or turn them so they cook evenly.

Air-dried ham. Place the slices of ham on a non-stick baking mat or greaseproof paper, on a baking tray. Make sure it has a lip to keep any fat from spilling in your oven. Place another non-stick mat or piece of greaseproof paper on top of the ham and then another baking tray on top. Place in a preheated oven at 180C and cook for 20–30 minutes. Check often, and if there is too much fat on the tray tip away safely. Once they are golden and crisp remove from the oven. Take off the top tray and mat/paper and leave to cool slightly on the bottom tray. Once cooled remove to a wire rack to cool completely.

Sauce for pheasant. In a pan heat the rapeseed oil, put the bones in and fry until golden brown. Remove the bones and keep to one side in a bowl. Turn the heat down and add onion, carrot, thyme and mushrooms. Put a lid on the pan and sweat without colouring. Once translucent, put the bones back in, add Madeira and reduce by half. Add the brown stock and simmer until you have 200ml left. Pass through a fine sieve and keep warm.

Serving. The tortellini need to be reheated in boiling salted water for 90 seconds. The pheasant can go back into a non-stick pan to warm on the stove or in the oven. In the middle of your plate put a little cooked curly kale tossed in butter and black pepper, or a little buttered cabbage. Place three tortellini around the edge of your plate along with morel mushrooms. Cut pheasant breast in half and place on top of kale or cabbage and drizzle with sauce. Finish with air-dried ham laid across the top.

We're fortunate to live near to the coast.

There are numerous fishing villages through Devon and Cornwall from which local fishermen depart each day.

They work hard to bring the best possible catch to our shoreline, doing their best to preserve our oceans for future generations.

We cook with the seasons, making the most of whatever is in abundance in any given month.

There are perennial favourites, of course, and turbot, cod, monkfish, halibut, stonebass and salmon feature in the following pages.

Our intention is to bring out the best flavour of those primary ingredients, matching them to items which are complementary. We cook fish in a way that preserves its texture, whether that's the delicate flakes of stonebass, the juicy chunks of cod, or the robust, almost meaty, texture of monkfish.

Great fish is synonymous with Devon and Cornwall and we hope you enjoy our celebration of the flavours from the sea.

"We cook fish in a way that preserves its texture, whether that's the delicate flakes of a stonebass, the juicy chunks of cod, or the robust, almost meaty, texture of monkfish."

Pan-fried stonebass with lentils, coriander, smoked bacon and lobster fritter

SERVES 4

4 × 150g–200g stonebass fillets
50ml rapeseed oil
25g unsalted butter
8 rashers thinly sliced smoked bacon, rind removed
Small bunch micro-coriander
Lobster weighing approximately 500g–600g
100g tempura flour (for a gluten-free version use 70g gluten-free plain flour and 30g gluten-free self-raising flour)
180ml fizzy water

Lentils
50ml rapeseed oil
100g lentil du Puy
1 onion, finely diced
1 carrot, peeled and finely diced
1 bayleaf
1 sprig of thyme
1 tsp ground cumin
500ml chicken stock

Lentils. Heat the oil in a frying pan, add onion, carrot, thyme and bayleaf, cover with a lid and sweat. When soft, add the lentils, cumin, stock, salt and pepper then simmer until cooked. Take off the heat and keep warm.

Smoked bacon. This is an optional extra. Place the rashers between two silicone mats or lightly greased greaseproof paper and then place between two baking trays. The bottom one should have a slight lip to keep any oil from spilling into the oven. Place something heavy on top of the top baking tray and cook at 180C for about 10 minutes. Check regularly and tip off any excess oil. You want the end result to be golden and crisp. Cooking time will depend on individual ovens. Once cooked, cool on a wire rack.

Lobster fritters. Bring a pan of salted water to the boil. Before you put the lobster in you will see a cross on top of its head. Push the tip of a cooks' knife into this to kill the lobster. Put the lobster into the water and cook for five minutes. Take out and place into ice-cold water to stop the lobster over-cooking. When cold, drain well.

Remove the head from the tail. Remove the claws and then remove the meat from the claws and knuckles and put onto kitchen paper. They will be undercooked, which is what we want.

Remove the tail meat in one piece, snapping each section of the tail. Pull the meat out and put onto kitchen paper. Mix the flour with the fizzy water until smooth but do not overwork: keep the batter light.

Cut the lobster into 12 pieces, pass through the batter and deep-fry at 180C until golden brown and crisp.

Stonebass. Heat the oil in a non-stick frying pan and add the stonebass skin-side down. Hold down in the pan with a fish slice to keep the fillet flat against the pan, or it will curl up at the sides. Cook for three or four minutes until golden underneath and then flip the fish over and cook for a further two minutes. When almost cooked add the butter, let it sizzle and baste the top of the fish with it. When cooked squeeze a little lemon juice over it.

Serving. I like to serve this in a soup plate. Place the warmed lentils in first and put your stonebass on top. Arrange three fritters per portion around the plate. Dress the dish with micro-coriander. On this occasion, I've decided not to serve it with bacon; should you want to, simply balance whole rashers on the fish, or break into smaller pieces and scatter..

Poached fillet of turbot, tempura of oysters, lettuce and tarragon juices

SERVES 4

4 × 175g–200g turbot pieces
200ml fish stock
25g butter
Salt and pepper

Oyster and lettuce soup
2 medium English lettuce
25g unsalted butter
1 small onion, peeled and chopped
500ml fish stock
6 oysters
80ml double cream
1 tbsp parsley leaves

Tempura of oysters
12 oysters, removed from the shell and patted dry on kitchen paper
100g tempura flour (for a gluten-free version use 70g gluten-free plain flour and 30g gluten-free self-raising flour)
180ml fizzy water

Buttered 'Little Gem' lettuce
4 × Little Gems, cut in half and stalk removed
25g butter

Tarragon juices
50g butter
2 shallots, peeled and sliced
400ml sweet white wine
400ml fish stock
50ml double cream
2 large sprigs of tarragon
Additional 100g butter, for the end

Butter a suitable dish, season with salt and pepper and place turbot in. Cover with the stock. Cover with a lid or tin foil and bring to around 80C and cook for five to seven minutes. Do not let it boil.

Oyster and lettuce soup. Separate the lettuce leaves, remove the thick stalk, wash and pat dry. Melt butter in a saucepan, add the onion and cook gently until soft and without colour. Add the fish stock, boil and then simmer until the liquid has reduced to about 200ml. Add the cream and bring to the boil. Add the oysters and poach for a minute. Add the parsley then the lettuce quickly, stir and liquidise straight away. Pass through a fine sieve and keep warm.

Tempura of oysters. Mix the flour with the fizzy water, lightly until smooth. Pass the oysters through and deep fry at 180C until golden brown.

Buttered lettuce. Blanch the lettuce in salted boiling water until just tender. Warm up in the melted butter, season with salt and pepper and keep warm.

Tarragon juices. Heat the 50g of butter, add the shallots and cook until soft. Add the white wine and reduce by half. Add the stock and again reduce by half. Add the cream and tarragon. On a low heat, simmer gently and then whisk in the remaining butter. Season and add a squeeze of lemon juice.

Serving. Place the buttered lettuce in the centre of the dish and place the tempura of oysters around the outside. Garnish with some of the oyster and lettuce soup. Place the turbot onto the lettuce and drizzle with tarragon juices. You can also garnish with some sliced new potatoes, tomato dice and micro-tarragon leaves.

Pan-fried monkfish, parsnip puree, oxtail, bone marrow and red wine

SERVES 4

4 × 200g monkfish tails, filleted, skinned and membrane removed
50ml rapeseed oil
25g unsalted butter

Parsnip purée
200g parsnips, peeled, cored and chopped
150ml milk
100ml double cream
50g butter

Oxtail
50ml rapeseed oil
1 oxtail, jointed and cut into pieces
1 carrot, peeled and cut small
1 small onion, skinned and chopped small
1 celery stick
1 garlic clove
1 tbsp tomato purée
2 bayleaves
1 sprig of thyme
1 bottle red wine
2000ml brown stock

Bone marrow
12 × 2.5cm cuts of bone marrow
1000ml brown stock
Flour
Egg wash
Breadcrumbs
Tarragon

Season the monkfish with salt and pepper. Heat the oil in a non-stick frying pan, add the monkfish and cook over a medium heat until golden brown on one side. Turn over, add the butter and cook for a further three to four minutes. The fish should be only just cooked; it should feel a little stringy. Remove from the pan and allow to relax for five minutes.

Parsnip purée. Place parsnips in a pan with milk and cream, and cook on a low heat until the parsnips are soft. Put in a small food processor and blend until smooth, adding the butter a little at a time. Season with salt and pepper. Keep warm.

Oxtail. Heat the oil in a suitable pan and brown the oxtail pieces all over. When brown remove from the pan and keep to one side. Add the vegetables and herbs and put on the lid and sweat. When the vegetables are soft add the tomato purée and red wine and reduce until you have 200ml left. Add the stock and bring to the boil. Put the oxtail pieces back in but do not let the liquid boil. Cover the pan and cook in an oven at 150C or lower depending on your oven, until really tender, three to four hours as a rough guide.

When cooked allow to cool and pick the meat off the bone while still warm. Remove any fat and cartilage as well. All you want is pure meat. (This can all be done days in advance. I cook about 10 tails at once. When the meat has been picked off I vac-pac into small pouches and freeze and take out as needed.)

Further reduce the liquid that is left until only 200ml remains. Pass through a fine sieve and keep warm until needed.

Bone marrow. Allow the marrow to reach room temperature – this should allow you to push the marrow out of the bones. Once out soak for 24 hours in cold water, frequently changing the water as you want to remove as much of the blood as possible.

In the brown stock poach the bone marrow gently until soft but still retaining its shape. This is best done by heating the stock first. When soft remove from the stock and allow to cool. Refrigerate to set again.

Pass the bone marrow through seasoned flour, beaten egg and breadcrumbs which has been blended with tarragon. Deep-fry at 180C until golden brown and the marrow is soft.

Serving. Place three spoons of parsnip purée on the plate and drag a teaspoon through each one to resemble a teardrop. In the middle of the plate place a little wilted spinach. Place some small pieces of oxtail around the outside with deep-fried bone marrow. Place the monkfish on top of the spinach and drizzle with red-wine juices.

Warm smoked salmon, pickled cucumber, yoghurt and caviar

SERVES 4

4 × 100g pieces of Cornish smoked salmon
4 new potatoes
1 cucumber
1 tsp sea salt
1 tsp white-wine vinegar
100g yoghurt
4 tsp caviar

Cucumber sauce
100ml white wine
100ml fish stock
200ml double cream
Skin of the cucumber

Garnish
Freshly cut mustard and cress
Tomato dice and chopped chives

Cook the new potatoes in simmering, salted water – keep slightly firm and cool in the water.

Cucumber. Peel the cucumber, keeping the skin to make the sauce.

Slice the cucumber lengthways, and remove the seeds with teaspoon. Slice it thinly lengthways. Place into a bowl with a little sea salt and leave to one side. The salt will draw out the water. After about 15 minutes tip off the water then add a teaspoon of sugar and white-wine vinegar to taste.

Sauce. Reduce the white wine by half, add the fish stock and again reduce by half, then add cream and bring to a boil. Liquidise the sauce with the reserved cucumber skin and pass through a fine sieve. Before you put the cucumber sauce onto the plate use a hand blender. This puts lots of air into the sauce and makes it light.

Serving. Put the salmon into a warm pan on the side of the stove, just to warm it through. Cut each potato into three slices and char-grill, then put into the pan with salmon to keep warm. Assemble the dish finishing with yoghurt, tomato dice, mustard and cress, cucumber fish sauce and caviar.

Pan-fried cod with spelt risotto and chicken wings

SERVES 4

4 × 150g–200g pieces cod – head end to middle of the loin would be best, scaled and pin-boned
50ml rapeseed oil
Salt and pepper

Chicken wings
12 chicken wings
25g sea salt
2 sprigs of thyme
1 clove garlic, finely chopped
300ml duck fat

Spelt risotto
1 small onion, peeled and finely diced
2 sprigs thyme, leaves stripped
2 cloves garlic
200g spelt risotto rice
100ml white wine
1000ml chicken stock, white or brown
50ml rapeseed oil
50g butter
Parmesan, grated

Morel mushrooms
28 fresh morel mushrooms
50g unsalted butter

Sesame and chicken juices
Trimmings from the wings
50ml rapeseed oil
2 sprigs of thyme
1 carrot, peeled and chopped small
1000ml brown stock
100ml Madeira
50ml sesame oil

Heat the oil in a non-stick pan, and place the fish in skin-side down. Cook over a medium heat for four or five minutes until the skin is crisp and golden in colour. If the fish is particularly thick, I make four or five incisions on the skin side at about 1cm–2cm deep – this allows the heat to penetrate into the middle of the fish. Turn over and carry on cooking for one or two minutes. Again you want to keep the fish just cooked. The different pieces may take different times to cook.

Chicken wings. With the chicken wings we just want the middle section; keep the two ends for the sauce. Place the middle sections in a bowl and toss with sea salt, garlic and thyme. Do this the day before and leave in the fridge overnight.

The next day rinse off the salt and herbs. Warm up the duck fat and put the chicken wings in and cook for an hour at 140C. The wings should be succulent and tender. When cool enough, remove the bones from the middle, keeping the wings whole.

For this recipe we just want to reheat them as they are but you could flour, eggwash and breadcrumb them, and then deep-fry until golden and crisp.

Spelt risotto. Twenty-four hours in advance, cover the spelt risotto with cold water and leave to soak overnight. Spelt risotto is not as absorbent as normal risotto, and it takes longer to cook.

Heat the oil, add the onion, garlic and thyme leaves, and sweat until soft, keeping it uncoloured. Add the drained spelt and cook for two minutes on a low heat. This lets the spelt crack and allows it to start cooking.

Add enough wine to cover the rice, and stir continuously. When the wine has been absorbed add a little more, just enough to cover, again stirring all the time and carrying on using the stock. Repeat this process until the spelt is *al dente* – tender but with a little bite; this can take up to 35 minutes. Just before you are ready to serve add the butter and a little grated parmesan and stir. It should be loose, and not too dry.

Morel mushrooms. Wash the morels in cold water to remove any dirt and pat dry with kitchen paper. Make sure they are completely dry. Heat the butter in a non-stick frying pan, add the morels and cook over a medium heat for around two minutes, depending on the size of the morels. Turn them every now and again so they cook evenly. Drain and keep warm.

Sesame and chicken juices. Heat the oil, add the chopped chicken wings that you have left, colour until golden brown, add carrot and thyme, put a lid on and sweat to allow carrots to soften. When soft, add Madeira and reduce by half, then add the brown stock and simmer until you have about 200ml left. Pass through a fine sieve and whisk in the sesame oil at the last minute. Keep warm.

Serving. Heat a little duck fat and warm up the chicken wings until golden brown. Pop the morels in the same pan and warm through.

Reheat the chicken juices and make sure you give them a good whisk to blend the sesame oil back in.

Place some risotto in the middle of the plate, arrange chicken wings and morels around the edge and put a piece of cod on top of the risotto. Drizzle with chicken juices.

You can garnish with asparagus spears, shelled broad beans or any other vegetable that you may like.

Pan-fried halibut with cauliflower, curry and mussels

SERVES 4

4 × 200g pieces of halibut
50ml rapeseed oil

Cauliflower purée
800g cauliflower, broken into florets
200ml milk
200ml cream
50g unsalted butter, diced

Mussels
25ml olive oil
1 small onion, peeled and chopped
1 bayleaf
1 clove garlic
500g mussels
250ml cider
1 sprig of thyme
1 stick of celery

Curry sauce
50ml rapeseed oil
1 shallot, peeled and chopped
1 tsp curry powder
1 bayleaf crushed
100ml white wine
200ml mussel/cider stock
50ml double cream
100ml milk

Tempura of cauliflower
12 small cauliflower florets
100g tempura flour (for a gluten-free version use 70g gluten-free plain flour and 30g gluten-free self-raising flour)
180ml fizzy water

Creamed leeks
1 leek, cleaned, in 1cm dice
100ml double cream

Season the halibut. Heat the rapeseed oil, and when hot add the butter. When it starts to fizz add the halibut and turn down the heat and cook for two or three minutes until golden. Turn over and cook for a further two minutes. It should be golden and just cooked. Squeeze some lemon juice over the halibut.

Cauliflower purée. Blanch the cauliflower in boiling salted water until just tender. Drain and add to the cream and milk. Bring to the boil, reduce heat and simmer gently until cauliflower is cooked. Put into a blender and blend until smooth. Purée, adding a little butter at a time. Check seasoning and keep warm.

Mussels. Heat the oil and add the onion, bayleaf, garlic, thyme and celery. Sweat until soft. Add washed and debearded mussels. Add the cider, put a lid on and steam for two to three minutes or until the mussel shells open. Throw away any mussels that do not open. Shell the remaining mussels. Strain the liquid through a fine sieve onto the mussels; this will keep them succulent.

Curry sauce. Heat the oil, put the shallot, bayleaf and thyme in and sweat until soft, then add the curry powder. Cook for about two minutes. Add the wine and reduce by half, then add stock and reduce by half again. Add the milk and cream, bring to the boil and simmer gently until the sauce thickens. Keep warm.

Tempura of cauliflower. Blanch the florets in boiling salted water and refresh in cold water. Mix the flour and water until a light batter is formed. Coat the florets and deep-fry at 200C until golden and crisp.

Creamed leeks. Blanch leeks in boiling salted water and refresh in cold water. Pat dry with kitchen paper. Heat the cream and reduce until thick, season with salt and pepper and stir in the leeks.

Serving. Arrange on your plate using your imagination, or as shown.

The South West's food scene is built on interesting characters. Few are as memorable as Derek and Judith, our local cheese suppliers.

The husband-and-wife team run a small, independent cheese shop in our local town, at Holsworthy. They do it for love, not money. They have reached a time in their life when they could easily put their feet up, sit back and relax. But they keep at it, day in and day out. They always have a joke or a story to tell us. They're fascinating people.

Derek and Judith opened their shop at the start of the Millennium. Food is their passion and they get a real buzz from discovering the best local cheeses and educating their customers.

We're regular visitors to their shop. During the spring, summer and autumn months, I cycle to Holsworthy to pick up my order. Derek is always very enthusiastic about what's on offer, encouraging me to taste whatever is new. He's a passionate photographer, too, and his shop is adorned with stunning photographs of the landscape and coast.

There was a time when British restaurants celebrated the best of French cheese. That always seemed odd to me. It felt like cheering on a rival football team. Why should we praise the virtues of a Gascony brie when several varieties that are just as good are made right here on our doorstep? What's the point of eating a North Country cheddar when we've got a number of great producers here in the South West.

Derek and Judith favour the best of our region. On a typical day, they might have a Devon Smoke, a Westcombe Traditional Somerset, a cumin-infused hard cheese from Cornwall, a West Country brie or a Pendragon buffalo's milk cheese. There's Curworthy Farm mini-truckles, Capricorn Somerset goat's cheese and much more besides. They find plenty of interesting varieties that you'll only find in specialist stores, such as an award-winning Cornish gouda, as well as a gouda with fenugreek.

Derek and Judith also know the stories behind the producers. The gouda, for instance, was created by a young cheesemaker who moved to the South West from continental Europe. His skills are first rate and his cheeses are popular among our customers.

Our customers really enjoy local cheeses – and so they should. They are made by a dedicated band of craftsmen and women who have a real pride in their work.

Cornish Crumbly
Whalesborough Farm Foods, Norton Barton, Launcells, Bude, Cornwall EX23 9LG - 01288 361317
Natural mould rind Pasteurised Milk, Vegetarian rennet
SERVE AT ROOM TEMPERATURE
UK CQ 536 EC

Spiced apricot, raisin and fig chutney

225g dried apricots, soaked overnight
120g dried figs, soaked overnight
350g onions, skinned
1 orange, finely grated and juiced
50g seedless raisins
225g light soft brown sugar
1 tsp English mustard
¼ tspn ground cinnamon
¼ tspn ground mixed spice
1 tsp salt
140ml malt vinegar

Drain the apricots and figs and chop roughly. Chop the onions finely. Put the onions, apricots and figs into a pan with the orange rind and juice. Add the remaining ingredients and bring slowly to the boil. Boil gently, stirring all the time, until the chutney is thick and well reduced and now excess liquid remains.

Pour the chutney into pre-heated jars, cover and seal in the usual way. Store in a cool dry place for two or three months to mature.

Pear chutney

750g pears, peeled, cored and roughly chopped
125g cooking apples, peeled and minced
½ tsp salt
250g tomatoes, peeled and chopped
125g onions, minced
125g sultanas
1 tbsp coarsely grated orange rind
2 oranges, juiced
300g sugar
½ tsp cinnamon
1 tsp nutmeg
1 tsp cayenne pepper
50g fresh ginger
300g white-wine vinegar
2 pinches of saffron

Put all of the ingredients, except the pears, into a large pan. Heat gently until the sugar has dissolved. Bring to the boil, stirring occasionally until the 'Jam' stage is reached on your sugar thermometer.
Add the pears and cook slightly. Put into jars while still hot.

Rhubarb and orange chutney

900g rhubarb, trimmed, washed and chopped
2 oranges, grated rind and juice
450g onions, skinned and chopped
900ml white-wine vinegar
900g light soft brown sugar
450g seedless raisins
1tsp mixed spice
1tbsp grain mustard
1 tbsp fresh ginger, grated

Put all the ingredients into a large wide-bottomed pan. Heat gently, stirring all the time until the sugar has dissolved. Bring to the boil, reduce the heat and simmer gently, stirring occasionally until the mixture is thick and pulpy and no excess liquid remains.

Put the chutney into pre-heated jars, cover and seal in the usual way. Store for two to three months to improve flavour.

Beetroot relish

350g raw large beetroot
50g onion, skinned
25g raisins
150ml red-wine vinegar
15ml grain mustard seeds
15ml horseradish
90ml light soft brown sugar

Wash the beetroot and wrap in foil. If you are doing a large amount, line a tray with tin foil, put beetroot in and cover with tin foil. Cook at 180C for two to three hours until tender. (Roasting the beetroots first helps to intensify the flavour and keeps them nice and dry. If the beetroots are too wet the cooking processes used to make your relish will be adversely effected.)

Leave the beetroot to cool, then skin and grate, either fine or coarse depending on your preference. I prefer coarse.

Thinly slice the onion.

Put the onion, raisins, vinegar, mustard, horseradish and sugar into a pan. Bring to the boil, stirring all the time. Simmer and reduce until a thick consistency is achieved. Add the grated beetroot. Spoon the mixture into pre-heated jars. Cover and seal in the usual way.

If using vacuum packed, pre-cooked beetroot, simply omit the initial roasting stage.

The philosophy behind our wine list is simple: we offer great variety at a price that people can afford. When it comes to wines, we buck the trend. We refuse to charge premium prices and prefer to provide a varied and good value list that matches our food.

We work with Charles Steevenson, an independent wine merchant who supplies restaurants and hotels throughout the South West.

Charles is a supremely knowledgeable man and has helped us to construct a list that offers customers variety – without being intimidating by offering too much choice.

We predominantly favour New World wines, though there is a happy mix of European too.

Charles Steevenson writes the whole list for us and advises us on what he thinks will work well with our food. He checks our menus regularly so that he can provide a competitive and good-value selection that perfectly matches our food.

Smoking Bishop

3 oranges
1 grapefruit
18 cloves
120g caster sugar
1 bottle red wine
½ bottle port
1 cinnamon stick, broken into pieces
1 tsp mace
1 tsp allspice
60g fresh ginger, peeled and grated into a cloth and squeezed to release the juice.

This is a type of mulled wine, punch or wassail. It was very popular in Victorian England at Christmas time. It appears in Dickens's *A Christmas Carol*.

There is a persistent myth, although wholly unsupported, that the name come from the shape of the traditional bowl shaped like a bishop's mitre, and that in this form it was served in medieval guildhalls and universities.

I have my theory as to why it was called Smoking Bishop, and maybe you will have your own!

Wash whole fruit and oven bake until golden brown. Don't go too far or the end result will be bitter.

Stud the fruit with the cloves. Put fruit into a large saucepan, add sugar, red wine (but not the port), cinnamon, mace, allspice and ginger juice. Cover with a lid or cling film and leave in a warm place overnight.

Next day, remove the fruit and cut in half. Squeeze the juice into the wine, discarding the skins. Add the port and heat gently. Do not boil – bring up to about 85C. Pass through a fine sieve, and store in a Kilner jar in the fridge.

To serve, warm gently.

The painted Friesians on the old wooden sign at Trekillick Farm are misleading – for farmers Pauline and Colin Dyer have an impressive herd of 250 Jersey cows.

The 'girls' are given love and affection by Pauline, Colin and their son, Mike, before they deliver milk to Trewithen Dairy.

The Dyer family don't only keep a dairy herd. In recent times they have diversified by bottling spring water from a borehole on their farm. Cornish Water is as pure as the driven snow and is popular with our guests.

"I only drink water," laughs Colin. "I'm an aquaholic. It's a good job I don't have to pay for it."

The family's Jerseys are showered with attention.

"They are all individuals," says Mike. "They all have their own personality and character. They are friendly creatures. We know each one of them.

"People imagine farmers simply have animals and don't get to know them. But we know all of our girls. They are a pedigree herd, so we know where they came from and how to look after them."

The Jerseys at Trekillick Farm lead lives that are much longer than those led by livestock on other dairy farms. While the life expectancy of a Friesian might be six or seven years, Pauline's and Colin's cattle live for almost double that.

They begin to produce milk at the age of two and reach maturity at the age of six, enjoying another six years of life after that.

"We're in tune with Mother Nature," says Pauline. "The Jerseys are well looked after and we breed from the herd, so we introduce new livestock every couple of years.

"The water that we have is deliciously fresh and pure. On the surface, it might seem that we're very traditional farmers, doing this in the old-fashioned way. But we have diversified in recent times to give people a true taste of Cornwall."

“I only drink water,” laughs Colin. “I’m an aquaholic. It’s a good job I don’t have to pay for it.”

From the side of the road, Holsworthy Ales' brewery doesn't look much.

It's tucked away far from view, on an unprepossessing industrial unit.

But step inside and it's a different story.

The rich, summery smell of hops fills the air. Clouds of steam provide mellow vapours, hinting at the delicious ales that will soon be bottled.

Brewer Dave is proud of his operation. He pays attention to detail, making sure each of his hand-crafted ales hits the spot with drinkers.

Dave is one of many artisanal producers who put their heart and soul into their produce.

He goes about his work with a smile on his face.

"I adore what I do," he says. "And I'm constantly looking for new ideas. I love experimenting and designing delicious ales that slip down perfectly."

Dave's sense of humour comes through in the names for his ales. There are classics, like Make Me Hoppy, Sun Shine and Muck 'n' Straw.

Then there are the one-off ales, like Bee Merry, or Bizzy Buzzy, which are sweetened with honey. Tamar Black and Conker King are perennial favourites and new ales are constantly appearing.

"As well as hops, grain and water, I'll use different aromatics to give my ales a distinctive flavour," he adds.

Like many Devonshire producers, Dave goes the extra mile. He chills his ales for two weeks after they've been brewed, so that they are in perfect condition when they reach drinkers.

"Not everybody lets the ales rest in the way that I do," says Dave. "But that's one of the ways to ensure a premium product. It takes a little longer and costs a little bit more, but the taste makes it worth it."

Cheers Dave, mine's a pint.

TAMAR BLACK
HOLSWORTHY ALES
CONKER KING
Autumn Ale
Alc 3.9%
HOLSWORTHY ALES
TRADITIONAL METHODS | GREAT BEER
BIZZY BUZZY
HOLSWORTHY ALES
SUN SHINE
Summer Ale
Alc 4.0%
HOLSWORTHY ALES
TRADITIONAL METHODS | GREAT BEER
MUCK N STRAW
BEE MERRY
Honey Stout
Alc 6.0%
HOLSWORTHY ALES
TRADITIONAL METHODS | GREAT BEER
MAKE ME HOPPY
Alc 4.7%
a springy hoppy ale
HOLSWORTHY ALES

SWEET

Bottling is a process which has been used since time immemorial. It's a great way to preserve fruits because the sterile, airtight jars help to kill yeasts and moulds that are already present in the food. The seals also prevent other bacteria from entering the jars. There are two ways of heating the jars: in a water bath or in a pressure cooker. They must be sealed while still hot.

PACKING THE FRUIT

The fruit should be packed tightly and wedged in place without squashing or bruising. The closer you can pack the fruit the better, as it shrinks during the process.

WATER BATH METHOD

This is the method that I use. It requires a pan that is 5cm deeper than the height of your jars, a thermometer and tongs.

Pack the jars with fruit, then fill with cold syrup, close the lid and secure the clip. Place the glass jars in the pan with a tea towel in the bottom, this stops the glass making contact with the metal of the pan and conducting too much heat.

Cover the jars with cold water and place the pan onto a low heat. I like to bring the water up to 83C over a 90-minute period and then hold for 20 minutes at that temperature.

After 20 minutes, very carefully remove the jars from the water. The jars will be very fragile. Leave to cool on a cooling rack.

When the jars are cool, test for a good seal by turning the jars upside down. If the seal is not good the liquid will seep out.

Syrup for bottled fruit

FILLS A 1-LITRE JAR

225g sugar
600ml water
1 bayleaf, crushed
1 cinnamon stick, split
2 star anise, in small pieces
5 cloves
1 vanilla pod, split
5 juniper berries, split
5 green cardamom pods, crushed
1 orange, zest and juice
1 lemon, zest and juice

Dissolve the sugar in 300ml of the water. Boil for one minute then add the rest of the water; this allows the syrup to cool a lot more quickly, as it needs to be cold when it goes onto the fruit. Add the spices, lemon and orange – you can play around with these, depending on what you like. For instance, you might want to add fresh ginger.

- Strawberries: 1.2kg
- Pineapple: Three medium-sized pineapples, peeled and cut into eight lengthways.
- Rhubarb: 1.4kg, peeled and cut into 5cm lengths.
- Plums: 1.5kg, halved and stoned.

Store unopened jars in a cool, dark place and they will keep for up to six months. Once opened, refrigerate.

Raspberry jam

What's not to like about homemade jams and marmalade?

A slice of my granary bread, toasted and still hot with a big knob of West Country butter, topped with lashings of homemade jam . . . Wow! That's how all days should start.

My advice after years of making jams is that the sugar cooks more quickly and the jam reaches its desired temperature when using smaller quantities. If you cook in bulk, it seems to take forever for the jam to set.

The maximum weight of fruit I would go to is 900g, but I have bigger pans and faster gases than home cooks might. If I were cooking at home, I would make jam in 450g batches.

Chef's tip. It might cost a little extra, but I always use preserving sugar for my jams and marmalades. It acts as a safety net.

900g raspberries
900g preserving sugar with pectin
1 lemon, rind and juice

Put the fruit and lemon into a pan and simmer very gently – be careful, I find that raspberries can stick very quickly – for about 20 minutes until the fruit is soft.

Add the sugar, then leave on a low heat stirring occasionally until the sugar has dissolved. Turn up the heat and boil rapidly. Always check to make sure the fruit has not stuck to the pan.

When the 'JAM' stage on your thermometer is reached, take off the heat and allow to cool.

Remove any scum and pot in the usual way.

Strawberry jam

MAKES ABOUT 450g

450g strawberries
450g preserving sugar with pectin
1 lemon, juiced and rind

Hull the strawberries and cut in half if very large. Place the strawberries and lemon in a suitable-sized pan and put on a low heat. Cook gently until soft. Add the sugar, stirring occasionally still on a low heat, until the sugar has dissolved. Turn up the heat and boil rapidly until 'JAM' is reached on your sugar thermometer.

Take off the heat and allow to cool for 15 minutes. Remove any scum, pot and cover in the usual way.

Chef's tip. The only time to make jam is during the summer months when English Strawberries are at their best. There are some real beauties grown in the Tamar Valley.

Kiwi conserve

MAKES AROUND 1.5kg

900g Kiwi fruit
900g preserving sugar
2 lemons, juice and rind

Peel the Kiwi fruits. Cut each into about eight, you could also slice thickly. Place in a bowl in layers with the sugar. Cover and leave for 24 hours.

Put all the ingredients into a wide-bottomed pan and set on a low heat until the sugar has dissolved. Turn up the heat and boil rapidly for five minutes. Make sure you stir just occasionally to make sure the sugar is not catching, or use a jam thermometer until it reaches the 'JAM' stage.

Leave to cool for 15 minutes, remove any scum, pot and cover in the usual way.

Chef's tip. The most common variety of Kiwi that we see is the Hayward variety. Other varieties are Gold, Jingold, Kiwi Berry and Red.

They are in season at different times of the year, depending on where they are grown. Between October and April they are imported from Greece and Italy. From April to November they are imported from New Zealand and Chile. Kiwi plants are either male or female of which the Hayward variety is borne to female.

Peach and lemon jam

600g peaches
4 cardamom pods (crushed)
3 tbsp orange juice
2 lemon, juice and rind
700g preserving sugar

Wash and peel the fruit, then slice it into a large bowl. Tie the stones in a muslin bag with the crushed cardamoms.

Put the peaches, orange juice, lemon zest and the muslin bag into a suitable pan. Simmer gently for about 20 minutes or until the fruit is soft. Add the sugar and put onto a low heat, stirring occasionally and dissolve the sugar.

Once the sugar has dissolved boil until 'JAM' is reached on your sugar thermometer. Remove from the heat and stir in the lemon juice.

Remove the muslin and squeeze all the juice from it.

Let it stand and then jar in the usual way.

Ginger marmalade

RECIPE AS FOR SEVILLE MARMALADE (see opposite)

Add:
225g preserved ginger, shredded
40ml ginger juice

To make the ginger juice, peel the ginger using large pieces, which are easier to hold. Grate on a coarse grater, straight into a piece of muslin. Once all grated, fold up the edges of your muslin and squeeze all of the juice out. Throw away the fibrous ginger and keep the juice. If you have too much juice place in a container in the fridge for the next batch.

Add the ginger and juice to the marmalade mixture once you take it off the heat when setting point is reached.

Chef's tip. You get beautiful flavours with this method, without all the rough fibres. The original recipe that I had, required putting the ginger in before cooking the sugar to setting point. I prefer mine to go in at the end. Try both ways and see which you prefer.

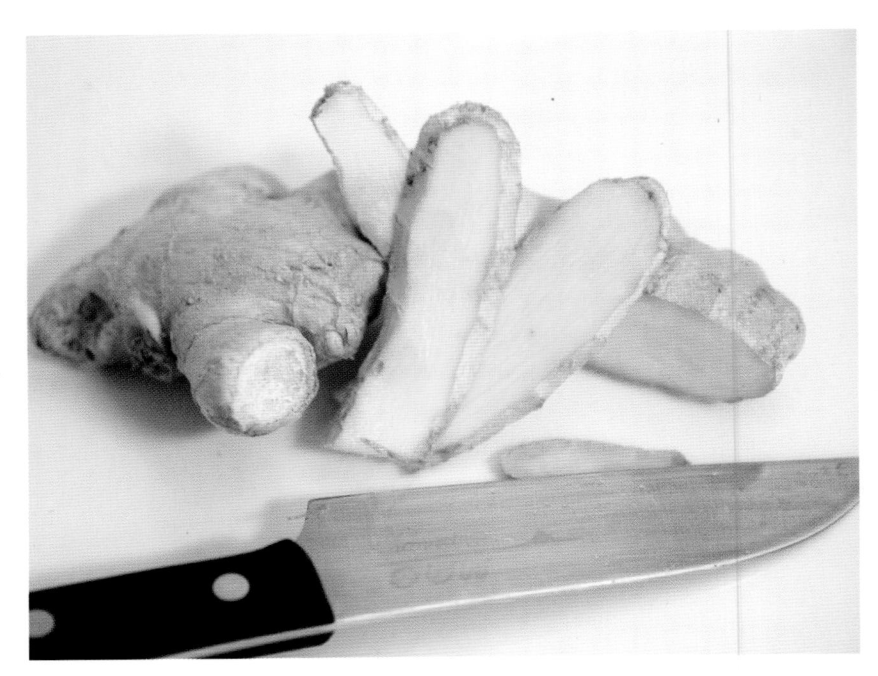

Seville marmalade

MAKES ABOUT 4.5KG

1.4kg Seville oranges, washed
3 lemons, juice
2.7kg preserving sugar

Halve the oranges and squeeze out the juice and pips. Remove any extra membrane. Tie the pips and the membrane in a piece of muslin.

Slice the orange peel thinly or thickly as preferred. Put the sliced peel, orange juice and muslin into a thick-bottomed pan with 3.5 litres of water. Simmer gently for about two hours or until the peel is really soft and the liquid is reduced by half. Remove the muslin bag, squeeze well, and let all the juice run back into the pan.

Add the sugar. Heat gently, stirring until the sugar has dissolved. Boil rapidly until 'JAM' is reached on your thermometer – about 15 minutes. Remove scum, pot and cover in pre-heated jars.

VARIATION: WHISKEY MARMALADE. Follow the recipe as above. When the setting point is reached, remove any scum then carefully stir in 150ml whiskey. Leave to stand for 15 minutes, then stir to distribute the peel. Pot and cover in the usual way.

Summer pudding terrine

450g–900g mixed summer fruits, fresh or frozen
3 gelatine leaves, soaked in cold water
1 orange, zest and juice
1 orange, segmented
170g caster sugar
¼ lemon, zest and juice
100ml white wine
13 slices of medium-sliced white bread

This 'Desserts' section will be many people's favourite. As a nation I think the majority of us have a sweet tooth. When I left college, I wanted to become a pastry chef but my first head chef told me that I was far more valuable to him in the main kitchen. After that I didn't pursue pastry and apart from my two years at South Devon Technical College I am self-taught. I must admit that I prefer the comfort of puddings, so the winter months suit my style more than the summer months, when desserts benefit from being lighter.

Line a 2lb terrine mould with cling film with enough to fold over the top when ready.

Cook all the fruit with orange zest and juice, lemon zest and juice, white wine and caster sugar until just soft. Add the orange segments.

Take off the heat and add the gelatine. Strain the fruit through a colander or sieve and keep the juice to one side. Remove the crusts from the bread and, one at a time, pass each slice through the juice and line the mould. Slightly overlap the edges of the slices lining the sides and the bottom.

Half fill the mould with the fruit, put a layer of soaked bread down the middle and then put the remaining fruit in on top. Finish the top with a final layer of soaked bread. Fold the cling film over the top.

Put a tray or something similar on top of the mould and weigh down just enough to compact it but not to squeeze everything out. Refrigerate overnight.

Turn out the terrine, cut a slice and serve. I use sugared fresh berries, raspberry sauce and, of course, clotted cream. But you could also serve with vanilla ice-cream, red berries, yoghurt sorbet or pouring cream.

Treacle tart

Sweet pastry
60g butter
125g plain flour
35g icing sugar, sieved
Pinch of salt
1 egg yolk
12ml cold water

Filling
600g golden syrup
160g fresh white breadcrumbs (they must be fresh to absorb the syrup)
1½ lemons, zest and juice
½ tsp ground ginger
½ tsp ground mixed spice – alternatively you can use Chinese five-spice powder

Pastry. Soften the butter using the paddle on your machine or with a spoon in a bowl. Add flour, salt, sugar and mix at speed 1 to almost the crumb stage. Add water and egg yolk. Mix, and once it all comes together stop the machine.

Turn out onto your work surface and work until a smooth paste is formed – but don't overwork it as that can lead to shrinkage. Wrap in cling film and refrigerate for 30 minutes.

Line an 18cm tart tin with a removable base by brushing it with butter and dusting it with flour. Turn over and shake out any excess flour.

Roll out the pastry and line the tin, then fork the bottom. Line the pastry with greaseproof paper and baking beans, and cook at 180C for about 12 minutes.

Take out of the oven, remove the greaseproof and baking beans, and put back into the oven for a further seven minutes or until lightly coloured. Take out and put to one side.

Filling. Warm the golden syrup, lemon zest and juice and spices in a sauce pan. Mix in the breadcrumbs and then pour into your pastry case. Cook in the oven at 160C for about 20 minutes. Once cooked remove from the oven and let stand for a while to set. Serve hot or cold.

Tasting of chocolate

SERVES 6

Dark chocolate ice-cream (see page 122)
Salted caramel doughnut (pages 118–119 for doughnuts, and page 123 for salted caramel)

Chocolate mousse
100ml double cream
40g milk chocolate
1 dsp glucose
1 dsp water
½ gelatine leaf

Chocolate sauce – I have to make this in a big batch, but it's worth it as it keeps well in an airtight jar in the fridge
70ml cream
125ml milk
160g dark chocolate
25g sugar
15g butter

Toffee sauce – again, I make a large batch but it keeps well in the fridge. Scale back if you wish
100g light soft brown sugar
100g golden syrup
75g butter
250g tin evaporated milk
150ml double cream

Honeycomb (pages 126–129)
200ml double cream, whipped

Pear and chocolate crumble
500g pears in syrup, cut up small
Toffee sauce (see above)
30 milk chocolate buttons, or chopped-up Flake bar or chopped chocolate
70g unsalted butter
70g light soft brown sugar
100g strong flour
30g ground almonds

Ice-cream. Follow the instructions on page 122.

Salted caramel doughnut. Make the doughnut and when deep-fried pass through cinnamon sugar.

Sundae. Put the water and glucose in a small, thick-bottomed pan on a low heat. Let the glucose dissolve. Soak the gelatine in cold water. When the glucose has dissolved add the gelatine and chocolate. Allow to melt. Take off the heat and keep warm.

Whip the cream to 'half-whip' and fold the chocolate mixture into the cream. Mix thoroughly; the glucose will keep it smooth. Before adding the chocolate mix to the cream make sure it is nice and smooth. If it looks like it is beginning to set, warm it on a low heat. You may need a drop of hot water from the kettle.

Divide between six shot glasses and put in the fridge to set. Once set, remove from the fridge and build up your sundaes. Have all of your other components out ready to use: chocolate sauce, toffee sauce, whipped cream and crushed honeycomb. Build up the layers of your sundae by alternating all of these two or three times – or however you fancy. Place in the fridge until ready to serve.

Pear and chocolate crumble. Have six small ramekins ready. Divide the chopped pear between them. Put some toffee sauce and chocolate buttons on top of the pear. Mix the sugar, flour and ground almonds and rub in the butter to form the crumble topping. Fill the ramekins with the crumble mix and cook in a preheated oven at 200C for seven or eight minutes. Take out and keep warm.

Serving. Once you have each item prepared and ready arrange on your chosen plate and finish with a quenelle of Devon clotted cream on top of the crumble.

Hot spiced apple and clove soufflé

SERVES 6

450g prepared apples, peeled, cored and sliced – I like Braeburn or Royal Gala
5 cloves
1 tsp mixed spice
2 tsp honey, set or clear
200ml cider
30ml calvados
10g cornflour
6 egg whites, at room temperature
60g caster sugar
Melted butter for ramekins

Pre-heat your oven to 200C.

Put the apples into a pan with cloves, mixed spice, honey and cider. Cook on a low heat until the apples are soft and the cider reduced by half. When cooked, put the apple mixture into a food processor and purée until smooth and the cloves broken up.

Pour the mixture back into the pan. Mix the cornflour and calvados together and pour into the apple mixture, stir and boil for two minutes.

Pour the mixture into a bowl, cover with a plate or cling film and keep at room temperature.

Lightly brush the insides of six ramekins with melted butter, making sure you cover the whole surface. Put into the fridge to set.

Whisk the egg whites until very soft peaks are formed. Whisk in the sugar, still trying to keep at soft peak. Do not overwhisk or else when they cook they will turn to water or be grainy.

Whisk a third of the whites into the apple purée until completely incorporated (this gets the two different textures used to each other), then carefully fold in the remaining whites. I use a whisk to do this but some people prefer to use a spatula. Whatever you use, do not knock any of the air out of the whites.

Remove the ramekins from the fridge, and brush with butter again (this traps a thin layer of air). Fill the first ramekin with caster sugar and rotate to coat the entire surface, then tip the sugar into the next ramekin and repeat until all six are sugared.

Fill each ramekin with soufflé mixture then smooth over the top and make sure that there is no mixture hanging out over the edges of the mould.

Cook in your pre-heated oven for seven or eight minutes. You may need to play with timings depending on your oven.

Once cooked, remove from the oven, dust with icing sugar and serve immediately with a shot of warm Smoking Bishop (page 93) and liquorice ice-cream (page 120).

Iced mint parfait

SERVES 4

Parfait
10 egg yolks
4 whole eggs
250g caster sugar
1000ml double cream, whipped
1 box After Eight mints
20ml crème de menthe

Mini doughnuts
See page 117

Gratin
5 egg yolks
125g sugar
50ml crème de cassis
125g double cream, whipped

Popcorn
100g honey
100g butter
100g sugar
1 tsp bicarbonate of soda
Popcorn

To garnish
Red berry coulis
Quartered strawberries
Thai basil leaves

Parfait. Put the After Eight mints into the freezer and leave until hard. When frozen put into a food processor and grind to a fine powder. Whisk eggs, egg yolks and sugar into a sabayon over a water bath until the ribbon stage is achieved. Once thick, remove and keep whisking until cold.

Gently fold in the whipped double cream, slowly add the crème de menthe and finally fold in the After Eight powder. Gently pour into stainless steel dariole moulds and freeze.

Gratin mix. Whisk egg yolks, sugar and crème de cassis into a sabayon over a water bath until the ribbon stage is achieved. Take off the heat and whisk until cold, then fold in whipped double cream. Keep in the fridge.

Toffee popcorn. Make some plain popcorn with a popcorn machine. Place honey, butter and sugar into a pan over a low heat, and when dissolved turn up the heat and cook until it reaches the hard-ball stage.

Take off the heat, add bicarbonate of soda and stir in the popcorn. Spread the popcorn on baking sheets and dry out in the oven at 125C for 30 minutes, turning every 10 minutes. When cool, dip in melted white chocolate.

Mini doughnuts. Follow the instructions on page 117. For four servings, you will need 36 discs of bread, 12 having the centres removed. Use lemon curd as your filling (also page 117).

Assembly. Place the raspberries on your plate, spoon over a little of the gratin mix and use a blowtorch to turn golden. Assemble as shown.

Chef's tip. I have tried making the parfait in smaller quantities but it just seems lighter when making this amount. This mix makes about 24 dariole moulds. Use the four you need and keep the rest for next time.

Chilli pineapple with pineapple-and-black-pepper sorbet

SERVES 6

200ml water
60g sugar
1 vanilla pod, split with seeds scraped out
4 cloves
4 green cardamoms, split
2 tsp ginger juice
1 tbsp sweet chilli sauce
1 medium pineapple, peeled
6 scoops of pineapple-and-black-pepper sorbet, (pages 124–125)

Bring the sugar and water to the boil, turn the heat down and add vanilla seeds, cloves and cardamoms. Simmer for 10 minutes and remove from heat.

Add the ginger juice and the chilli sauce. Set aside to cool.

Slice the pineapple as thinly as you can – almost paper thin. Arrange 12 slices on your plate, cover with a thin layer of the syrup and leave to marinade for 10 minutes.

Serving. Put a scoop of sorbet into the middle of the plate and dress with micro-coriander.

Doughnuts

SERVES 6

6 slices medium-sliced white bread – you can use gluten-free
1 egg white
Chosen filling
Sugar to dust

Plain batter
80g tempura flour – for the gluten-free version use 50g gluten-free plain flour and 30g gluten-free self-raising flour
180ml ginger beer, cider or lemonade

Chocolate batter
80g tempura flour
20g cocoa powder
180ml ginger beer, cider or lemonade

Lemon curd (should you want it)
6 lemons, zest and juice
12 eggs, beaten
750g butter, chopped into small cubes
600g caster sugar

See overleaf for pictures.

Cut three 5cm circles out of each slice of bread. In one of each batch of three circles cut a 4cm hole in the middle, and keep just the outer ring.

Dip a whole disc in egg white (very quickly as you don't want it to go soggy). The egg white acts like a glue and holds the bread together. Place a ring on top and fill the hole with your chosen filling. Dip another disc in egg white and place on the top. Gently pick it up and give a little squeeze to make sure it is all stuck together.

Repeat to make five more doughnuts.

Gently mix your batter, then pass each doughnut through the batter, coating completely, and deep-fry at 180C for seven minutes. Turn every couple of minutes to get an even finish.

Drain on kitchen paper and pass through sugar.

You can have many variations – here are a few of my favourites:

- apple, cinnamon sugar, plain batter.
- lemon curd, ginger sugar, plain batter.
- salted caramel, plain sugar, chocolate batter.
- strawberry jam, plain sugar, plain batter.
- peanut butter, nutmeg sugar, chocolate batter.
- mincemeat, allspice sugar, plain batter.

These are only suggestions. Have a play around and see what you come up with. Don't be afraid to experiment!

Lemon curd. Place all of the ingredients into a bowl that will sit over a pan of simmering water – but not touching the water. Stir continuously to keep all of the ingredients mixed together. The mixture is cooked when it starts to thicken.

Remove from the heat, being careful not to scald yourself on the water in the pan underneath. Put into jars and keep in the fridge.

Doughnuts – method

Doughnuts – batter and fillings

The origins of ice cream can be traced back to at least the 4th century BC. Early records show Emperor Nero (A.D. 37-68) ordered ice to be brought from the mountains and combined with fruit toppings.

King Tang (A.D. 618-697) of China had a method of creating ice and milk concoctions. Ice cream was likely to have come to Europe from China. Over time, like everything else, recipes evolved. Ices, sherbets and milk ices were served in fashionable Italian and French Royal Courts. Similar desserts were also popularised by several famous Americans.

George Washington and Thomas Jefferson served ice cream to their guests. In 1700 the Governor of Maryland was recorded as having served his guests. In 1774 a caterer in London called Philip Lenzi, announced in a New York newspaper that he would be offering for sale various confections including ice creams.

The first Ice Cream parlour was opened in USA in 1776 in New York. American Colonists were the first to use the term "Ice Cream". The name came from the phrase "Iced Cream". That was similar to "Iced Tea".

Ice cream is such a popular dessert and it is so easy to make that I'd encourage you to invest in a machine. Those available at the bottom end of the market, which contain a bowl that requires freezing, don't really provide you with good value for money. But you can pick up a decent ice cream machine for around £250, which should yield exceptional results for many years. The recipes here will make a substantial quantity which you can freeze and keep. You can, of course, scale back the recipes to make smaller quantities.

Vanilla ice-cream

Sorbet syrup
1500g caster sugar
250g glucose
1280ml water

Ice-cream
1760ml double cream
560ml milk
340g sugar
15 eggs, yolks only
4 vanilla pods, split and scraped
425ml sorbet syrup (see above)

Sorbet syrup. Place all the syrup ingredients into a pan and put onto a low heat until the sugar has dissolved. Turn up the heat and boil gently for 20 minutes. Cool down and store in an airtight jar for use as required.

Ice-cream. Boil 1200ml of double cream with the milk and vanilla pods. Mix together the egg yolks and sugar until thick and airy, either by hand or machine. Once the cream and milk have boiled, pour onto the egg yolks and sugar, continuing to stir as you pour. Mix well. Return to the pan and cook gently until the mix coats the back of a spoon. If you cook it too quickly, you will scramble the eggs. Leave for 24 hours. After 24 hours, mix in the additional 560ml double cream and sorbet syrup and churn in the usual way.

NB: Do not leave the egg yolks uncovered as they will form a skin and you will be left with little yellow flecks in your ice cream. When you add the sugar to the egg yolks mix together straight away.

Chocolate ice-cream

1000ml milk
150ml double cream
5 eggs
350g sugar
100g dark chocolate couverture
100g cocoa powder

Whisk the eggs and the sugar till pale and creamy. Mix the cocoa powder, milk, cream and cocoa powder in a pan and bring to the boil. Cook slowly for about five minutes.

When it has boiled, pour onto the eggs and sugar while whisking. Melt the chocolate and add to the mixture. Strain and chill and fridge for 24 hours. Churn in the normal way.

Prune and Armagnac ice-cream

1000ml vanilla ice-cream mix (page 120)
500g prunes – see recipe for breakfast prunes (page 145)
300ml prune juice
200ml Armagnac
500ml double cream

Mix all the ingredients together and churn in the usual way.

Chef's tip. I keep the chopped prunes back and put them in when the ice-cream is almost set as my machine would break them up if they go in at the beginning.

Liquorice and meringue ice-cream

1000ml vanilla ice-cream mix (page 120)
568ml double cream
340ml sorbet syrup
Liquorice, cut into small pieces
Meringues, either homemade or shop-bought

Add the double cream to your batch of vanilla ice-cream. Add the sorbet syrup and churn in the usual way.

Just before it has finished churning, add some cut liquorice and crushed meringues, tailoring the amounts to suit your taste.

Peanut brittle ice-cream

142ml water
225g caster sugar
225g unsalted peanuts
½ quantity of vanilla ice-cream mixture (page 120)

Line a tray with a non-stick baking mat or oiled parchment for the brittle. Into a suitable saucepan put the sugar and water on a low heat. When the sugar has dissolved, turn up the heat and cook the sugar until a nice golden colour is reached. Take off the heat and stir in the peanuts. Turn out onto your prepared tray – being very careful as the sugar will be very hot. Allow to cool. Once cooled, break into small pieces with a rolling pin or pulsed through a food processor. Keep to one side.

Churn the vanilla ice-cream and when almost set mix the brittle in and give a few more turns. Put into a suitable container and freeze.

Chef's tip. Make sure your brittle pieces are not too big. If they are too large it will be very hard to ball in an ice-cream scoop.

Baileys ice-cream

575ml milk
450ml double cream
125ml Baileys
1 vanilla pod
3 whole eggs
4 egg yolks
225g sugar
2 tsp vanilla extract

Put the milk, cream, split vanilla pod and vanilla essence into a pan and bring to the boil.

Mix together the eggs, egg yolks and sugar until pale and creamy in texture. Once the milk and cream mixture has boiled, pour over the eggs, stir and mix well.

Return all the mixture to the pan and cook until the mixture coats the back of a spoon. Once cooked put into a container in the fridge for 24 hours.

After 24 hours add the Baileys and churn. Put into a suitable container and freeze.

Salted caramel

250g caster sugar
25ml water
150ml double cream
150g butter, small dice
Maldon sea salt

Salted caramel is something every chef and home cook should be able to make. It has a variety of uses: I like to fill my homemade doughnuts with it (see page 117).

Place the sugar and water into a suitable pan, on a low heat. When the sugar has dissolved turn up the heat. When a dark colour is reached – ensuring it is not too dark, otherwise it will be bitter – remove from the heat.

Add the cream carefully – adding cold liquid to very hot liquid can cause the mixture to bubble vigorously. Then add in the butter but do not let it melt, you must keep stirring it in so that milk and cream don't separate. Finally add the Maldon sea salt to taste.

Sorbet is a frozen dessert made from sweetened water flavoured with fruit, wine or liquor. Sorbet is often confused with Italian ice-cream.

The ingredients that you add to your sorbet will alter its consistency; for instance, alcohol lowers the freezing temperature, resulting in a softer texture.

I use equal quantities of sorbet syrup to whatever flavour I am making. The recipe for sorbet syrup is on page 120. For the best results, use an ice-cream mixer. If you do not have one, you can freeze it, though you need to remove it from the freezer regularly and mash with the back of a fork, to break down the ice crystals, before returning to freeze.

These recipes will make enough to keep and freeze, though you can scale back the quantities if you wish to make a smaller batch.

Lime sorbet

1kg lime purée
1000ml sorbet syrup (page 120)

Mix both ingredients together. Churn in the usual way.

Yoghurt sorbet

1kg Greek yoghurt – you can use a supermarket brand such as Total, though I actually use a yoghurt made by our local dairy, Trewithen, which is more acidic.
1000ml sorbet syrup (page 120)
3 tbsp lemon juice

Mix all the ingredients together. Churn and freeze in the usual way.

Rhubarb sorbet

1000ml sorbet syrup (page 120)
1kg rhubarb
4 tbsp lemon juice
100ml Stones ginger wine

I like to use forced rhubarb from Yorkshire; it is young and tender and doesn't need to be peeled.

Cut up the rhubarb into 1.5cm lengths. Put the rhubarb and sorbet syrup into a pan and bring to the boil. Simmer until cooked. Liquidise and pass through a sieve. Put into a bowl and cool in the fridge. Add lemon juice and ginger wine and churn in the usual way.

Put into a container suitable for freezing.

Chef's tip. I like to cut all fruit for sorbets quite small, so that it cooks quickly and retains its colour.

Blackberry sorbet

1000ml sorbet syrup (page 120)
1 kg blackberries
4 tbsp lemon juice

The dark colour of blackberry sorbet looks great. Blackberries are only available for a short time at the very end of summer, or start of autumn, so if you have a glut from your hedgerows it's well worth freezing them for future use.

Rinse the blackberries in cold water. Place on kitchen paper and leave to dry. Put the blackberries into a pan with the sorbet syrup. Bring to the boil and then simmer for two to three minutes. Liquidise and pass through a sieve. Put into a suitable container and put in the fridge to cool. Add the lemon juice and churn in the usual way. Put in a container suitable for freezing.

Apple and honey sorbet

250ml sorbet syrup (page 120)
675g Granny Smith apples
2 lemons, juiced
125ml water
1 tbsp honey

Peel, quarter and core the apples. Slice the apples straight away, put into a pan with the sorbet syrup and cook until soft. Liquidise the apples and pass through a fine sieve. Then add the water, honey and lemon juice. Put into a suitable container and into the fridge to cool. Once cold churn in the usual way.

Rice Krispies

- 4 tbsp caster sugar
- 2 tbsp clear honey or golden syrup
- 125g butter
- 150g Rice Krispies

Line a tray with cling film. Put the sugar, honey or golden syrup and butter into a saucepan and gently melt. Simmer on a low heat until golden, which should take three or four minutes.

Add Rice Krispies and mix well. Pour the mixture into a tray and press to flatten. Cover with cling film and leave in a cool place to set for a couple of hours.

Turn out of the tray and remove cling film. If you like you can melt some chocolate and cover the top or drizzle over.

Honeycomb

350g caster sugar
2 tbsp glucose
100ml clear honey
100ml water
1½ tsp bicarbonate of soda

Grease your baking tray so that it is ready.

Place sugar, honey, glucose and water into a heavy-based pan and bring to the boil.

When the mixture reaches 160C (light caramel) remove it from the heat.

Add the bicarbonate of soda and stir quickly. Be careful when doing this as the mixture will expand and the sugar is very hot! Immediately pour it into your greased tray and leave to cool and set.

Once it is set, break the honeycomb into small pieces. I store mine in an airtight Kilner jar and it will keep for two weeks – if it doesn't get eaten first!

Chocolate and mincemeat brownie

200g good quality dark chocolate, chopped
330g soft brown sugar
250g butter, cubed, plus extra for greasing
4 large eggs, beaten
200g plain flour
¼ tsp baking powder
35g cocoa powder
200g mincemeat
1 tsp mixed spice
100g chopped hazelnuts

Preheat oven to 180C. Grease a 22cm square brownie tin and line the base with baking paper. Put chocolate, sugar and butter in pan over a low heat until the ingredients have melted and combined. Remove and put into a bowl to cool a little.

Mix the beaten eggs in thoroughly. Add flour, baking powder, cocoa, mincemeat, mixed spice and nuts. Stir to combine all of the ingredients. Spread into the tin and bake in a preheated oven for approximately 25 minutes or until set. Allow to cool in the tin. Dust with cocoa powder. Cut and serve.

Mother-in-law's shortbread

330g plain flour
220g butter, soft
110g caster sugar

Put all of the ingredients into a mixer and mix until well bound. Roll out the mixture and cut into your preferred size of rounds. Put onto either a greased baking tray or onto a silicone mat on a tray.

Bake at 170C–180C for six or seven minutes or until golden brown. Transfer to a wire rack to cool and sprinkle with caster sugar. For an alternative add 55g of ground amaretti to the mix and follow as above.

Turkish delight

450g caster sugar
150ml rosewater
150ml water
10 leaves gelatine, soaked in cold water
1 lemon, juice only
1 tsp baking powder
Red food colouring – I use strawberry essence

Boil caster sugar, rosewater and water for eight minutes. Take off the heat and add soaked gelatine, lemon juice and baking powder. Pour into a tray lined with cling film. Allow to set for 24 hours.

Remove from tray, peel off the cling film and cut into your preferred shape and size. Just before serving pass through a mixture of two-thirds icing sugar, one-third cornflour.

White chocolate and cranberry fudge

750g sugar
250g glucose
375g double cream
160g butter, small dice
375g white chocolate, chopped
170g dried cranberries

Heat the cream, sugar and glucose in a pan over a low heat until the sugar and glucose have dissolved. Turn up the heat, keep stirring and make sure it does not stick to the pan. Cook to the hard ball stage (227C).

Take the pan off the heat and whisk in the butter, chocolate and cranberries. Transfer mixture to a tray lined with cling film. Allow to set, ideally for 24 hours.

Once set remove from tray, remove cling film and cut into preferred size.

White chocolate and Cointreau truffles

3 oranges, zest only
1 tbsp water
1 tbsp sorbet syrup – (page 120)
1 glass of Cointreau
284ml double cream
790g white chocolate, chopped

In a heavy-bottomed pan bring the orange zest, water and sorbet syrup to the boil. Add the Cointreau and cream and bring back to the boil. Remove from the heat and stir in the white chocolate until melted and all combined.

Place into a container and, when cold, put in the fridge to fully set. Shape into balls of desired size and dip into melted dark chocolate. Allow to set.

Using some melted white chocolate in a small piping bag, drizzle over the top. Alternatively, after dipping in melted dark chocolate, you could roll in some cocoa powder or finely chopped nuts.

Toffee popcorn

200g popcorn
115g butter
115g golden syrup/honey
115g light soft brown sugar
2 flat tsp bicarbonate of soda

Cook the popcorn in a popcorn machine (every household should have one!). If not, it can be cooked in a covered bowl in the microwave.

In a heavy-based pan melt the butter, golden syrup or honey and sugar on a low heat. Once dissolved turn up the heat and cook to 120C. Remove from the heat and stir in the bicarbonate of soda – be careful as the sugar will be very hot and the mixture will expand.

Stir in the popcorn so it is evenly covered with the toffee mix. Place the popcorn onto a baking tray with a non-stick mat and cook for 10 minutes at 120C. Take out and stir around, then put back in the oven for another 10 minutes. Repeat this. When it is ready it will be a nice golden brown.

Turn the popcorn out on to an oiled tray and allow to cool enough to handle. Separate the popcorn and allow to cool fully. When completely cold store in an airtight container.

SIMPLE

Afternoon tea is one of life's gentle pleasures. Sumptuous cakes and refreshing drinks combine to create a delicious occasion.

The custom of afternoon tea is believed to date back to Anna, 7th Duchess of Bedford, in the early 19th century. In those days, dinner was served as late as 9pm, which left the Duchess hungry in the afternoon. She took to ordering tea, bread and butter in her room and so began the tradition. Afternoon tea is typically served between 3pm and 5pm and can include savoury finger-sized sandwiches. That is followed by scones with jam and clotted cream – and here in Devon we have the world's very best. We also serve a selection of family-favourite cakes. The food is just a part of it. Having time to sit down with friends and family to eat and relax makes for the perfect afternoon.

Scones

500g plain flour
Pinch of salt
2 tsp bicarbonate of soda
4½ tsp cream of tartar
75g unsalted butter, diced
300ml milk
1 egg, beaten

For fruit scones, add 100g of sultanas into the mix

Preheat oven to 180C. Sift the flour, salt, bicarbonate of soda and cream of tartar into a large bowl. Rub the butter into this and then add the milk. Mix until just combined.

Turn out onto a floured work surface and knead lightly to form a dough. Roll out to about 3cm thickness and cut out the scones.

Place on a baking tray with non-stick mat and brush tops with beaten egg. Cook for approximately 12 minutes until golden and risen.

Lemon drizzle cake

170g self-raising flour
115ml sunflower oil
170g caster sugar
4 lemons, rind only
1 tsp baking powder
4 tbsp milk
2 eggs

For drizzle
Juice of 2 lemons
85g caster sugar

Grease and line the base of a 20cm cake tin. Mix all of the cake ingredients together until they look sloppy. Bake in the oven at 180C for about 20 minutes, until springy to the touch.

While the cake is cooking, mix the lemon juice and sugar for the drizzle. When the cake is cooked remove from the oven and prick all over the top with a skewer. Pour over the lemon and sugar mix. Allow cake to cool in the tin.

Mother-in-law's chocolate cake

225g plain flour
2 tsp baking powder
½ tsp bicarbonate of soda
Pinch salt
3 eggs
55g cooking chocolate
284ml milk
140g butter
280g soft dark brown sugar
1 tbsp treacle
1 tsp vanilla essence

Chocolate ganache icing
50g dark chocolate
25g unsalted butter
12g double cream
40g mini marshmallows

Sift the flour, baking powder, bicarbonate of soda and salt together. Put the chocolate and milk into a small pan and heat gently over a low heat. Stir until the chocolate has melted, remove from the heat and allow to cool.

Cream the butter and sugar until pale and fluffy. Beat in the eggs, one at a time with a little flour. Mix in the treacle and essence, and then fold in the rest of the flour mix. Now add the milk and chocolate, then mix to a batter-like consistency.

Have two deep, bottom-lined, sponge tins prepared. Pour the mixture into the tins and cook at 180C for about 35 minutes or until cooked.

Ganache icing. Melt the chocolate and butter in a bowl over a pan of simmering water. Keep mixing it together while it's melting. Once melted take off the heat and mix in the cream. Allow to cool and then pour over the cake. Decorate with marshmallows.

Fruit cake

675g butter
675g soft brown sugar
12 eggs
900g plain flour
8 level tsp baking powder
Pinch of salt
1.8kg brandy-soaked fruit, including 450g each of sultanas, currants and raisins and 225g each of glace cherries and mixed peel
1 tsp allspice
1 tsp cinnamon
2 tbsp black treacle

Grease and line three 900g loaf tins and preheat oven to 160C.

Cream the sugar and butter until light and fluffy. Slowly add the eggs. Mix in the flour, baking powder, salt and spices, and then the soaked fruit. Pour mix into the tins and cook for about one hour.

Banana bread

450g bananas
450g caster sugar
450g plain flour
21g baking powder
Pinch of salt
4 eggs, beaten
55ml vegetable oil
142ml milk

Preheat oven to 180C. Grease and line three 450g loaf tins. Beat the sugar, bananas and salt until smooth. Beat in the eggs, one at a time. Add the flour and baking powder and mix in. Finally add the vegetable oil and milk.

Pour into prepared tins and cook for approximately 25 minutes.

Carrot cake

175g light soft brown sugar
200g self-raising flour
2 eggs
150ml sunflower oil
3 tsp of mixed spice
1 tsp ground ginger
1 tsp bicarbonate of soda
300g carrots, peeled and grated
1 orange, zest and juice
120g sultanas
50g pecans, chopped
50g walnuts, chopped

Icing
200g Philadelphia soft cheese
1 orange, zest only
50g icing sugar

Preheat the oven to 170C and grease and line a 900g loaf tin. Put the sugar, eggs and oil in a bowl and whisk with an electric hand whisk for two to three minutes or until the sugar has dissolved. Sift in the flour, spices and bicarbonate of soda and fold in.

Now add all the remaining ingredients and mix well. Pour the mix into the prepared tin and level off the top with the back of a spoon. Cook for 30 minutes.

Icing. Mix all ingredients together and spread over the top of your cooled cake.

Smoked haddock and prawn crumble

SERVES 4

1 small onion, peeled and chopped
900g smoked haddock, cut into small chunks
300g raw king prawns
25g butter
150ml white wine
Salt and pepper
75g crème fraîche
1 tsp cornflour, blended with a little milk
Sprinkle of saffron

Crumble
75g ground almonds
75g plain flour
50g butter, diced
Parsley, roughly chopped

Melt the butter in a large saucepan over a low heat and cook the onion for about 10 minutes, stirring frequently.

Add the wine, cover and simmer for another 10 minutes. Season the haddock and add to the pan. Cover and cook for five minutes. Stir the prawns in and cook for a further five minutes.

Using a slotted spoon remove the mix from the saucepan and put into an ovenproof dish, leaving the juices in the bottom of the pan. Stir the crème fraîche, saffron and cornflour mix into the juices until smooth and then pour over the fish. Leave to cool for 30 minutes.

Put all of the crumble ingredients into a bowl and rub together until they resemble breadcrumbs. Cover the fish with the crumble and bake for 25 minutes at 180C until golden.

Serve with a nice green salad. This dish is also nice using salmon, in which case just leave out the saffron.

Moussaka

SERVES 4

Aubergine, 8 large length-wise slices
500g minced lamb
2 cloves garlic, crushed
2 small courgettes, grated
150g feta
70g breadcrumbs
Salt and pepper
1 tbsp rapeseed oil
250g ricotta
100g mozzarella
Dried oregano

Preheat oven to 180C. Place half of the aubergine slices onto a lined baking tray and brush with a little oil.

Mix the lamb, garlic, courgettes, feta, breadcrumbs, a sprinkle of oregano, salt and pepper in a bowl until fully combined. Divide the meat mix between four aubergine slices and press on top. Place the other four aubergine slices on the top of the meat, brush with a little oil, spread ricotta over the top and then grate the mozzarella and finish with another sprinkle of oregano.

Bake in the preheated oven for around 45 minutes until nice and golden on the top and the meat is cooked.

We like this served with a simple salad and a slice of good bread.

Steak-and-kidney pudding

SERVES 6

50ml rapeseed oil
675g chuck steak, in 2.5cm cubes
225g ox kidney, in 2.5cm cubes
1 onion, peeled and finely chopped
Salt and pepper
1 tsp thyme leaves
2 tbsp plain flour, singed in the oven to give it a nutty flavour (it also less glutinous than if you were using normal flour)
200ml fresh brown stock
Worcester sauce
1 tbsp tomato purée

For the suet pastry – this mix will suffice for a 600ml/1 pint bowl
140g flour
85g fresh white breadcrumbs
110g shredded suet
½ tsp salt
1 level tsp baking powder

Steak mix. Place the steak and kidney into a large bowl, season with salt and pepper and thyme leaves. Heat the oil in a thick-bottomed pan and fry the meat until golden brown all over. Remove from the pan and keep to on side.

Add two tablespoons of oil and the onion to the pan, put a lid on and sweat. When the onions are soft and translucent, remove the lid, add the tomato purée and mix. Add the singed flour, then add the brown stock and as much Worcester sauce as you would like. Add the meat and mix.

Cover with a circle of greaseproof paper and place into the oven for about two hours at 150C. I always make this the day before I need it, giving it chance to rest and the flavours to develop.

Suet crust. Mix all the dry ingredients together, and moisten with cold water to form a dough. Do not overwork, and keep the suet in its original shape. (When it steams and melts it leaves little air pockets.)

Butter a pudding bowl and lightly dust with flour. Line it with two thirds of your dough. Fill the mould with the steak mix. Roll the remaining dough to fit the top. Moisten the edges of the pudding bowl pastry with water and place the lid on. Press down to form a good seal.

Place a circle of buttered greaseproof paper on the top, cover with tin foil with a folded crease and tie around the rim with string nice and tight: we don't want any water getting in because it would make the pudding stodgy and heavy.

Steam the pudding for about two hours in a steamer (or you can cook it in the oven in you prefer at 150C).

Turn out carefully onto a serving dish.

Chef's tip. You can make individual puddings using smaller moulds. This mix should do six 115g moulds.

Filo-topped salmon

SERVES 4

4 salmon fillets
200g Philadelphia with salmon
4 sheets filo pastry
Melted butter
Salad and new potatoes to serve

Place the salmon fillets onto tin foil in a baking tray. Top the fillets with a good layer of Philadelphia.

Lay out a sheet of filo pastry, brush with melted butter and fold in half, brush with melted butter again and then scrunch to the size of a fillet. Put it on top of the cheese, pressing lightly it so it stays on top. Repeat for all fillets.

Bake in a moderate oven for approximately 20 minutes until the salmon is cooked and the filo nice and golden. Serve with a green salad and new potatoes.

Variations. Use plain Philadelphia or instead of filo press a seed mix on to the top for a nice crunch.

Chicken, ham and mushroom pie

SERVES 4

4 chicken breasts, skin removed and cut into 2cm cubes
200g bacon lardons
200g button mushrooms
Seasoned flour
200ml chicken stock
1 small glass white wine
200g crème fraîche
1 red onion, peeled and chopped
1 packet ready-rolled puff pastry
50ml rapeseed oil

Fry the onion until soft then add lardons and cook. Remove and set aside.

Toss the chicken in seasoned flour and add to the pan and cook through. Then add onion and bacon back into the pan. Add the stock and wine and gently simmer for 10 minutes.

In a separate pan, fry the mushrooms in a little oil then add to the chicken mix. Cook gently for a further 10 minutes. Stir in the crème fraîche and transfer to an ovenproof dish.

Cut the pastry into individual portion sizes and put onto a greased baking sheet. Put both pastry and chicken into a preheated oven at 180C and cook until pastry is golden (approximately 20 minutes).

Remove from the oven and serve chicken mix onto plates, topping each one with pastry. Serve with new or roasted potatoes and some seasonal vegetables.

"Dusted with brown sugar and infused with Drambuie, our porridge puts a real spring in the step of our guests."

Breakfast is the favourite meal for many of our guests, so we push the boat out and try to create flavours that excite.

I don't propose to write a recipe for our full English breakfast: people know what they like and how to cook it. There is a tried-and-tested formula and I don't deviate from it.

The ingredients for our full English are made right here on our doorstep.

Darren's eggs are laid a couple of miles from the door. His hens scratch around beneath trees, roaming freely before delivering eggs with golden-coloured yolks. The bacon and sausage comes from Sue and Malcolm. Their pigs lead extraordinarily happy lives, rooting for food in capacious pens on their farm. The flavours are a delight. Sue and Malcolm cure their own bacon, giving it an intensely savoury flavour, while the sausages are meaty and robust. They contain 83 per cent pork mixed with seasoning and a little ground rice, so that they are suitable for those on gluten-free diets.

We make our own bread and have shared our recipe with you on pages 30–35, while plenty of other bits and pieces are also locally made.

Of course, not everybody likes to start the day with such a large meal, so we offer a full range of toast and jams, using the recipes shared on pages 102–105, as well as croissants and other pastries.

Two of our most popular breakfast dishes are prunes and porridge.

People rave about our prunes, which I make myself. I've explained how in the recipe and urge you to give them a go. The porridge is similarly popular. Dusted with brown sugar and infused with Drambuie, it puts a real spring in the step of our guests.

Porridge

SERVES 1

40g Scott's porridge oats
250ml milk
1 tbsp double cream
1 dsp light soft brown sugar
Drambuie to taste

In a heavy-bottomed pan bring the milk to the boil, add the oats and stir. Cook for six minutes stirring continuously so that it doesn't stick to the pan.

When cooked, remove from heat and add Drambuie to taste.

Pour into your bowl, drizzle with the cream and sprinkle sugar on the top. Glaze under the grill until the sugar has melted. If you don't have a suitable grill a small blowtorch is good.

Prunes

1000ml orange juice
500g pitted prunes d'Agen
5 teabags
2 bayleaves
1 cinnamon stick
1 vanilla pod, split
6 cardamom pods
2 tbsp caster sugar
3 pieces star anise

Put all of the ingredients except the prunes into a heavy-bottomed pan. Put on a low heat to dissolve the sugar.

Turn up the heat and add the prunes. Bring to the boil and simmer gently for 20 minutes. Take off the heat and allow to cool completely.

Once cool pour into an airtight container and store in the fridge.

Rooms

The views from Blagdon Manor are impressive. On a sunny day, the undulating Devonshire hills stretch for more than 35 miles from the restaurant's sumptuous dining room.

But that's not the most impressive aspect of Blagdon. At least, that's what our guests tell us.

The hotel provides a home from home, where every last detail is taken care of. We're tucked away in rolling countryside and our restaurant with rooms has impressive heritage. A dwelling was listed in the *Doomsday Book* and the current buildings date back to the 17th century.

We have spent many years and invested heavily in refining and extending our guest rooms.

Our six en-suite bedrooms have been individually furnished to exude warmth and charm. The rooms are cosy, warm and inviting with hand-stitched soft furnishings and views to the gardens and beyond.

Buckhorn is a large superior room with a 6½ft four-poster bed. There is a seating area within the room with a lovely large window offering views to the south, overlooking terrace, conservatory, gardens and beyond to Dartmoor.

Clawton is a resplendent superior room on two levels with a 6ft leather bedstead with seating area. Two window seats facing south and east provide views over gardens and beyond to Dartmoor. The bathroom has a slipper bath positioned by the window with lovely views and there is a separate walk-in shower.

Larkworthy is a suite with a large split-level bedroom, with either a 6ft double bed or two 3ft twin beds. A separate sitting area leads to a large bathroom with a separate bath and there are views over the garden from its south-facing windows.

Ashwater is a standard double room with a 6ft double or two 3ft twin beds , views over garden to the east and an en-suite shower room, while Tetcott features a 6ft double bed, sloping ceilings and beams, a window looking to the west and an en-suite bathroom.

Finally, Quoditch is a smaller bedoorm with a window facing west over the gardens and beyond towards Bodmin Moor.

Our grounds are similarly resplendent, with manicured gardens extending to more than three acres. They are filled with herbaceous borders, seasonal flowers, a bowling-green-esque lawn and plenty of impressive horticultural features.

Inside, Blagdon has everything to make guests feel comfortable. Two dining rooms, a library, a sophisticated bar and a lounge give people plenty of space in which to relax. The dining rooms look over Yes Tor, on Dartmoor.

We are a dog-friendly restaurant with rooms, and travellers are likely to meet our own chocolate labs, Mace and Cassia better known as the Blagdon Spice Girls.

We are very much geared up for travellers looking for a home from home from which to enjoy Devonshire's stunning countryside amid peaceful, tranquil surrounds.

Index

Acknowledgements

Many years of hard work, long hours and determination rekindled our desire to return to the West Country. For both of us Blagdon Manor offers everything. It is our home and during your visit, it is your home from home.

Our story is not over, however, and as we look to the future new challenges lay on the horizon. We are excited and energised about what the coming years may hold.

Over the years we have had the privilege to work alongside some truly wonderful people, many of whom have become very dear friends. We could not have achieved our dreams on our own and we have so many people to thank for believing in us.

We are very lucky to have such a supportive team working with us. There are so many things to do that go unseen, which keeps Blagdon Manor a very special place.

- Ruth Carroll and Amanda Horsburgh – waitresses
- Gemma Marshall and Laura Falk – kitchen assistants
- Pearl Martyn, Vikki Moon, Lin Jennings and Jade Jennings – housekeepers
- Joss Carroll – builder
- Bill Maddock – handyman
- . . . and last but not least. both sets of our parents who help out in so many ways.

The South West has such an abundance of ingredients, which we take our time to source. Quality is of the utmost importance to us and to you.

- Charles Steevenson Wines – Tavistock
- Cornish Orchards – Duloe
- Holsworthy Ales – Clawton
- Just Water – Kirland
- MC Kelly – Copplestone
- Market Cheeses – Holsworthy
- Orchard Hen Farm – Ashwater
- Philip Warren & Son Butchers – Launceston
- Portland Shellfish – Portland
- St Austell Brewery – St Austell
- Seasonal Vegetable Co. – Clawton
- Tamar Fruiterers – Saltash
- Trewithen Dairy – Lostwithiel
- Wing of St Mawes – Indian Queens

And finally, our thanks go to the team who helped to create *From The Heart*: our designer Adam and photographer/writer/publisher, Andy.

TITANIC

QUICK SNACK
FEED ME

200833

animal